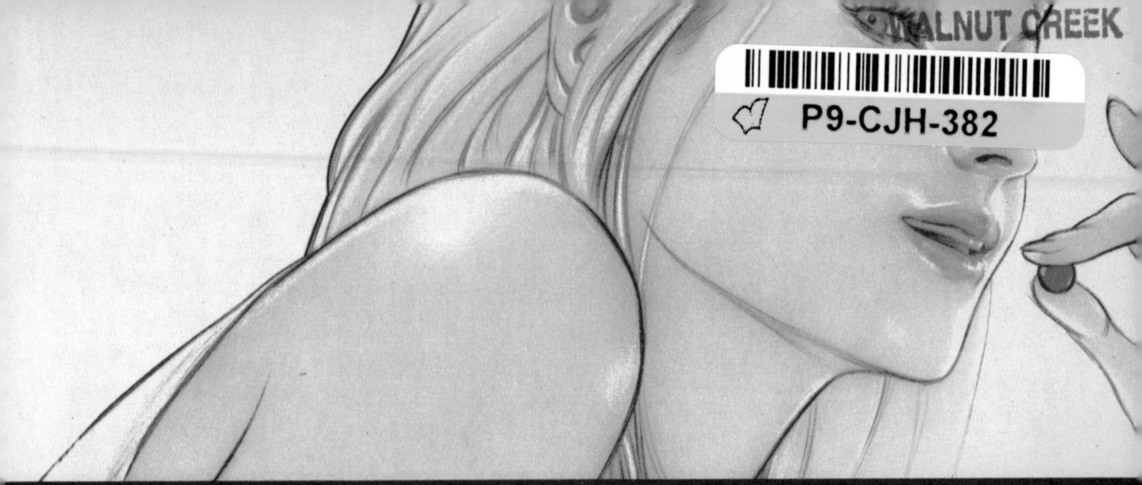

FABLES: WOLVES

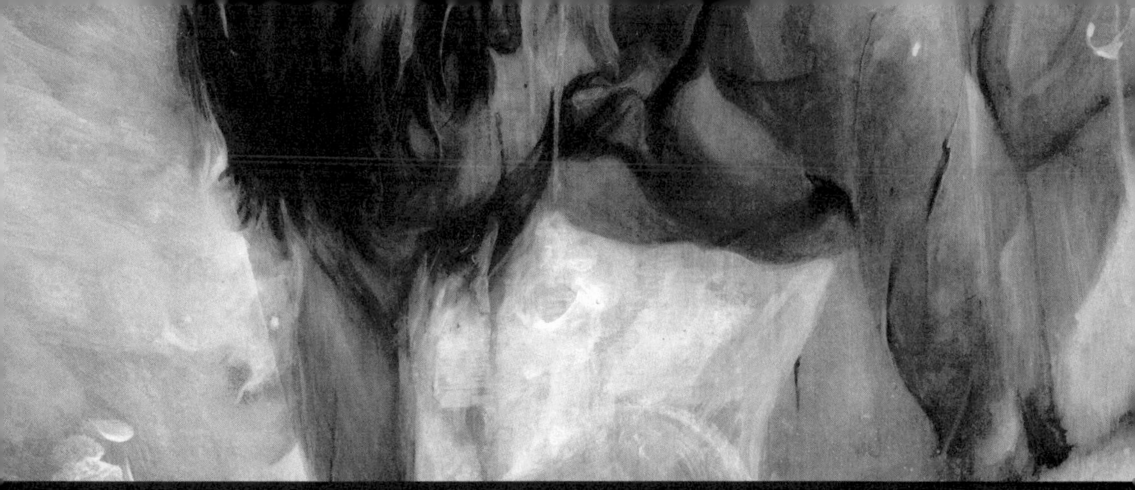

FABLES: WOLVES

FABLES CREATED BY BILL WILLINGHAM

Bill Willingham
writer

Mark Buckingham
Shawn McManus
pencillers

Steve Leialoha
Andrew Pepoy
Shawn McManus
inkers

Lee Loughridge
Daniel Vozzo
colorists

Todd Klein
letterer

James Jean
original series covers

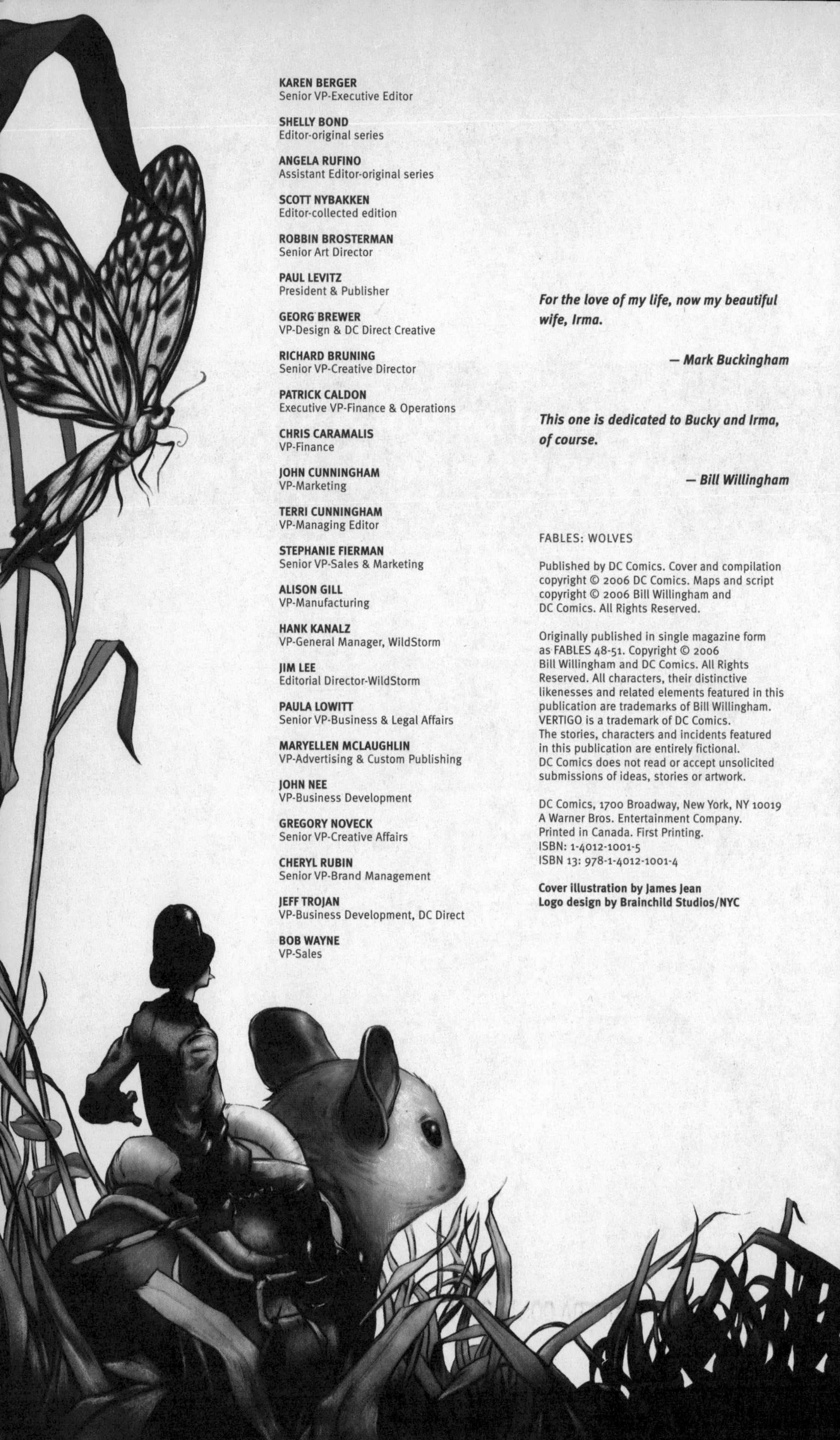

For the love of my life, now my beautiful wife, Irma.

— Mark Buckingham

This one is dedicated to Bucky and Irma, of course.

— Bill Willingham

FABLES: WOLVES

DC Comics, 1700 Broadway, New York, NY 10019
A Warner Bros. Entertainment Company.
Printed in Canada. First Printing.
ISBN: 1-4012-1001-5
ISBN 13: 978-1-4012-1001-4

Cover illustration by James Jean
Logo design by Brainchild Studios/NYC

Table of Contents

WHO'S WHO IN FABLETOWN

BIGBY WOLF

The former sheriff of Fabletown, but now off sulking in some hidden wolfy lair.

PRINCE CHARMING

He's the new mayor of Fabletown and w
he wasn't. It seems he enjoyed getting
job much more than doing the job.

MOWGLI

He was raised by wolves, but he's all grown up now and serving Fabletown as one of their secret agents, whom they call the Tourists.

ROSE RED

She's Snow's formerly wild-child twin sister who has settled down lately and now runs the Farm.

GEPPETTO

Recently revealed as the bloody-handed Adversary.

PINOCCHIO

Geppetto's first-carved son. He used to live in Fabletown but has recently returned to the homelands to live with his father.

THE STORY SO FAR

Some time ago, the Adversary's forces invaded Fabletown in the form of an army of wooden soldiers. The invasion was defeated, just barely, but it has always irked Prince Charming — the new mayor of Fabletown — that they never properly paid the Adversary back for his misdeeds. So Mayor Charming has worked out a plan of retribution against the Homelands

CINDERELLA

She serves our heroes as a spy at large, quite unknown to Fabletown's population, who imagine she's merely the bratty owner of the Glass Slipper Shoe Store.

SNOW WHITE

The former deputy mayor of Fabletown and mother of Bigby's seven cubs. She has to live on the Farm now, until her brood learns to pass as human.

THE LOST CUB

Bigby and Snow's invisible seventh child. He's just a puff of air who got into trouble at the Farm, so Snow had to send him away (hopefully) to find his father.

THE CUBS

Bigby's their father, Snow is their mother, and they're just a delightful pack of monsters.

MR. NORTH

He's the living North Wind and Bigby's estranged father. For the past few months he's been visiting his grandkids at the Farm.

BAGHEERA

He took part in the Animal Farm uprising and must continue doing hard time until Mowgli completes his secret mission to find Bigby.

BY LATE NOVEMBER I REACH THE SMALL PORT TOWN OF **PROVIDENIYA.** IT LIES ON RUSSIA'S CHUKOTKA PENINSULA, TOO CLOSE TO THE ARCTIC CIRCLE FOR MY COMFORT.
GOOD EVENING, CAPTAIN.

I WASN'T BRED FOR WINTER CLIMES.
IVANUSHIKA ZHELEZNOVA'S INTERNATIONAL CAPITALISM SAMOVAR
MAY I SIT?
NEW BEEF IS HERE

EVENING? IT IS BARELY **AFTERNOON,** YOUNG WESTERNER.
MAY I SHARE THIS WITH YOU, CAPTAIN? TAKE THE EDGE OFF THE COLD?

WOLVES
PART 1 OF 2
IN WHICH MOWGLI DRINKS IN A RUSSIAN BAR, RUNS INTO ONE DEAD END AFTER ANOTHER, AND PRACTICES A DEADLY FORM OF POLITICS.

I WON'T TURN DOWN FREE DRINKING.
SIT, YOUNG WESTERNER, SIT.
IS IT SO OBVIOUS WHERE I'M FROM?

OF COURSE. YOUR RUSSIAN IS ATROCIOUS. **BARELY** UNDERSTANDABLE.
AND WHO ELSE HAS MONEY FOR ENTIRE BOTTLES OF VODKA IN THE DEAD OF WINTER?

FAIR ENOUGH. TO YOUR CONTINUED GOOD HEALTH, SIR.
MAY I ASK YOU SOME QUESTIONS?
MMMM.

I TRACKED A MAN HERE. HE ARRIVED LAST SPRING, USING THE NAME **JOHN HOLBER,** BUT HE MAY HAVE CHANGED THAT AGAIN.
HE'S CHANGED IT OFTEN IN THE PAST YEAR OR SO.

SOUNDS LIKE SOMEONE WHO DOESN'T **WANT** TO BE FOUND.
TRUE. BUT IF HE KNEW WHAT NEWS I BRING, HE MIGHT DECIDE DIFFERENTLY.

I DON'T KNOW THIS MAN. IS HE A WESTERNER ALSO?
HE'S FROM AMERICA, I'M NOT.
BUT YES, NEITHER OF US IS FROM AROUND HERE.

HERE IS FOOD.
PLEASE ALSO PREPARE A **GENEROUS** PLATE AND DRINKS FOR ANYONE ELSE HERE WHO'S WILLING TO TALK TO ME.
I'M PAYING.

IF HE WAS EVER HERE, HE DIDN'T STAY LONG ENOUGH TO BE NOTICED.
YES. MY GUESS IS HE HOPPED A BOAT FROM HERE, BUT NONE OF THE BOAT CAPTAINS RECALL TAKING ANY FOREIGN PASSENGERS.

YOU SHOULD TALK TO THE AIR PILOTS. WE HAVE AN AIRSTRIP ACROSS THE BAY, NEAR THE MILITARY BASE.
I ALREADY HAVE, WITHOUT SUCCESS.

ENJOY THE DRINK, CAPTAIN.
PLEASE TELL YOUR COLLEAGUES THAT I HAVE GOOD AMERICAN DOLLARS FOR **ANYONE** WHO CAN BE OF HELP TO ME.

FABLETOWN'S FARM ANNEX IN UPSTATE NEW YORK.
SIT STILL, YOU HOOLIGANS.
WHY DO WE ALWAYS HAVE TO GET PICTURES TAKEN ALL THE TIME?

BECAUSE, WHEN YOU FINALLY MEET YOUR FATHER, HE'LL WANT TO SEE HOW EACH OF YOU LOOKED WHILE GROWING UP.
CHRISTMAS DADDY from:
DARIEN
DARE

BUT IT'S NOT CHRISTMAS YET, MOMMY.
IT'S CLOSE ENOUGH.
MERRY CHRISTMAS DADDY from:
BlosSom

SO WILL WE GET PRESENTS EARLY TOO?
NO.
CHRISTMAS DADDY from:
AMBROSE

DOES DADDY GET THE GIFTS WE SEND HIM?
OF COURSE.
CHRISTMAS from:
Winter

MR. SUNNYFLOWER SAYS DADDY GOBBLES PEOPLE UP.
MR. SUNFLOWER HAS ANGER ISSUES.
from:
CONNER

WILL HE EVER COME HOME?
SOMEDAY.
CHRISTMAS from:
Therese

OKAY, BABIES, THE TORTURE'S OVER FOR NOW. WE'RE DONE.
FINALLY!
YOU DIDN'T TAKE A CHRISTMAS PICTURE OF GRANDPA! HE CAN DRESS AS SANTA AGAIN!
GRANDPA *IS* SANTA, ISN'T HE, MOMMY?
DOES HAVING CHRISTMAS EARLY MEAN WE'RE SKIPPING THANKSGIVING, AUNTIE ROSE?
OF COURSE NOT, SILLY GOOSE.
MERRY CHRISTM
DAD
CAN WE CHANGE OUT OF OUR GOOD CLOTHES NOW?
CAN WE GO OUT AND PLAY?
IN A MINUTE, BUT I WANT YOU ALL TO SIT DOWN FIRST. WE STILL HAVE ONE IMPORTANT THING TO TALK ABOUT.
YOU HAVE A GROUP DECISION TO MAKE ABOUT FLYING AND CHANGING INTO WOLVES AND SUCH.

I SPENT THE LONG, COLD WINTER IN PROVIDENIYA, WHERE BIGBY'S TRAIL STOPPED COLD.
HE ARRIVED THERE AND NEVER LEFT. HE DIDN'T TAKE A BOAT, OR PLANE, OR TRAIN AWAY FROM THERE. NONE THAT I COULD FIND, ANYWAY.

NONE OF THE SUPPLY TRUCKS OR THE VERY FEW CAR OWNERS GAVE HIM A RIDE.
ИЧЕТ.

BUT NO ONE IN TOWN REMEMBERS EVER SEEING HIM, AND I STAYED LONG ENOUGH TO TALK TO EVERYONE.
HE SIMPLY DISAPPEARED.

ИЧЕТ! I SAID LAST MФИTH, I DФИ'T SEE THIS MAИ.

THEN IT OCCURRED TO ME I MIGHT BE ASKING THE WRONG PEOPLE.

THE CHUKOTKA PROVINCE IS MOSTLY WILD AND BARREN COUNTRY, STILL POPULATED BY MANY WILD BEASTS--WOLVES AMONG THEM.

AND EVEN MUNDY WOLVES ARE PART OF THE BROTHERHOOD. EVEN THEY KNOW THE RUDIMENTS OF MY FIRST TONGUE.

HOW IS IT A MAN COMES AMONG THE FREE PEOPLE, SPEAKING OUR LANGUAGE?
I AM MOWGLI OF THE SEEONEE WOLF PACK.
NONSENSE. YOU ARE MAN, NOT WOLF. GO AWAY, BEFORE WE GROW HUNGRY.

AM I TABIQUI, THE JACKAL, THAT YOU SPEAK SO TO ME?
NEVER!
I AM THE STRONG HUNTER, THE SWIFT RUNNER, SUBTLE TRACKER.

AND DEADLY KILLER--IF NEED BE.

PERHAPS SO, BUT YOU ARE NOT ONE OF *US*, SO WE'LL SPEAK NO FURTHER TO YOU.
THEN I'LL *BECOME* ONE OF YOU, IF THAT'S WHAT IT TAKES TO GET YOU TO ANSWER MY QUESTIONS.

POINT OUT YOUR LEADER, SO THAT I MAY SLAY HIM AND TAKE OVER RULE OF THIS PACK.
THIS ISN'T THE TIME FOR SUCH THINGS.

PAH!
YOU WILL NOT SLINK AWAY LIKE DISH-LICKING DOGS, FOR *THAT* IS NOT MY WILL.
THIS IS NOW A *KILLING* MATTER.

ONCE I'D PUT THE LEAD WOLF ON THE SPOT HE COULDN'T REFUSE MY CHALLENGE AND STILL HOPE TO KEEP THE RESPECT AND LOYALTY OF THE PACK.
TURN AND *FACE* ME, OLD WOLF.
IF YOU *INSIST* ON THROWING YOUR LIFE AWAY.

BUT WE WILL DO THIS IN THE PROPER MANNER--*TONIGHT* AT THE COUNCIL ROCK.
THERE I WILL TEAR AND REND YOU BENEATH MY *FANGS*.

AT THE SAME TIME AT THE FARM...
THIS IS THE HOUR OF PRIDE AND POWER, TALON AND TUSH AND CLAW.
OH, HEAR THE CALL!-- GOOD HUNTING ALL, THAT KEEP THE JUNGLE LAW!

IS THIS REALLY THE PLACE?
YEP. THIS IS THE VERY SPOT WHERE WICKED OLD SHERE KHAN FIRST STARTED HUNTING MOMMY.
AUNTIE ROSE CALLS HIM *LUNGRI*. I THINK THAT'S SUPPOSED TO BE A TIGER INSULT.

HE STALKED HER THROUGH THE TALL GRASS, FANGS BARED! CLAWS OUT!
BUT MOMMY WASN'T AFRAID.

SHE LED THE DEADLY TIGER TOWARDS THE HIGH HILLS, WHERE THE **GIANTS** USED TO SLEEP.
AND AUNTIE ROSE'S RAVEN CLARA TOO! WHEN SHE USED TO BE A DRAGON!
DO YOU THINK WE'LL REALLY FIND SHERE KHAN'S BODY?

OF **COURSE** WE WILL. ALL WE HAVE TO DO IS GO WHERE MOMMY WENT.
PROBABLY ONLY HIS BONES LEFT.

YYYEEEAARRRRGGGHHH!!

I'M THE DREAD TIGER'S GHOST AND I'M GOING TO **EAT YOU UP!**

AAAAAGHHH!

DARE

GRRRRRRRR!
GRRRRRR!
KILL IT!
BUT IT'S--
AUNTIE ROSE?
HAW HAW HAW HAW HAW HAW!
HEE HEE HEE HEE HEE!

I GOT YOU!
I GOT YOU SO GOOD!
NO FAIR!
THAT WAS A TERRIBLE THING TO DO!

TOO BAD, HELLIONS. YOU ALL HEARD THE DEAL: NONE OF YOU CAN LEAVE THE FARM UNTIL YOU PROVE YOU CAN GO A WHOLE MONTH WITHOUT FLYING OR CHANGING FROM HUMAN FORM.
SO FAR YOUR RECORD IS THREE DAYS.
BUT YOU CHEATED!

NOPE. TESTING'S PART OF THE DEAL.
YOU'RE STUCK HERE WITH ME UNTIL YOU DON'T AUTOMATICALLY WOLF-OUT OR FLY AWAY ANYTIME YOU'RE STARTLED.
THIS WAS MY FAVORITE SHIRT.

BUT I DIDN'T FLY OR CHANGE, AUNTIE ROSE.
ONLY BECAUSE YOU WERE TOO SCARED TO DO ANY-THING.
TOO BAD, AMBROSE. IT'S A GROUP PROPOSITION. THE WHOLE PACK SUCCEEDS OR FAILS TOGETHER.

THAT NIGHT THE FREE PEOPLE MET AT THE COUNCIL ROCK.
THE PACK IS ASSEMBLED AND TUKAR OUR LEADER IS HERE. LET MOWGLI THE CHALLENGER STEP FORWARD.
AFTER THE NEWBORN CUBS WERE INTRODUCED TO THE PACK, AND AFTER AN APPROPRIATE AMOUNT OF GOSSIP AMONG THE ADULTS, IT WAS TIME FOR THE BLOOD-LETTING.
PUT ASIDE YOUR THUNDER-MAKER AND STEEL FANG.
AND STRIP AWAY YOUR ODD COVERINGS.
WE AREN'T MEN, OR SCREECHING MONKEYS WHO USE TOOLS, AND DRESS IN SKINS NOT OUR OWN.
THE LAW OF THE PACK ALLOWS FOR NO WEAPONS BUT THE ONES YOU WERE BORN WITH.
NO PROTECTION BUT YOUR OWN FUR AND SKIN.
NO CHANCE OF BACKING OUT NOW.
THAT'S WHY I'LL SOON FEEL YOUR BONES GRINDING UNDER MY TEETH.

THE FREE PEOPLE AREN'T LIKE MEN, CONSTANTLY DITHERING AND REVISING.
MAYBE SO.
STATEMENTS BOLDLY MADE CAN'T BE LATER WITHDRAWN.
MAYBE NOT.
AS SOON AS I ISSUED MY CHALLENGE, IT WAS ORDAINED ONE OR BOTH OF US WOULD DIE BEFORE THE NIGHT ENDED.
HATEFUL MAN!
KILL YOU!

REND YOUR FLESH!
YIPE!
YAHH!
CHOMP!
YAAAAA-AAHHHH!

OOF!
ACK!
YUNTH!
HURRY, BROTHERS! WE'RE *MISSING* IT!
AAAAHHH!

YOOF!
IT WON'T LAST LONG NOW!

YYERRG!

SNAP!

NO, STAY BACK, BROTHERS. IT CAN'T END UNTIL...WAIT TO SEE WHICH ONE DIES FIRST.

I WON'T BE DYING TONIGHT.
TUKAR, ARE YOU STILL ALIVE?
FOR NOW.
YOUR BACK IS BROKEN-- ALONG WITH BOTH FORELEGS. YOU CAN NO LONGER HUNT. YOU CAN'T EVEN MOVE.
IF YOU PROMISE NOT TO BITE AT ME ANYMORE, I'LL COME OVER THERE AND FINISH YOU QUICKLY.
BITE, THOUGH, AND I'LL LEAVE YOU TO STARVE SLOWLY.
NO, IT'S OVER FOR ME. I'LL THANK YOU FOR A FINAL MERCY...
SNAP!

THERE.
NOW I'M THE LEADER OF THE PA--

AAAAAAACK.

THAT WAS A VERY LONG, UNCOMFORTABLE NIGHT. ANY CUB COULD HAVE FINISHED ME, BUT THAT ISN'T THE WAY OF THE FREE PEOPLE.
NO ONE WOULD TRY TO KILL ME UNTIL I WAS WELL ENOUGH TO BE PROPERLY CHALLENGED.

HE NEXT DAY I HIKED ALL TOO SLOWLY BACK INTO TOWN FOR MEDICAL HELP. IT WAS ANOTHER TWO WEEKS BEFORE I COULD REJOIN MY NEW PACK.
THE GOD OF WOLVES CAME LAST YEAR IN THE GREEN SEASON.
HE WAS A GIANT AMONG US.

HE DIDN'T CHALLENGE TUKAR FOR PACK LEADER, BECAUSE GODS DON'T NEED TO. WE SIMPLY DEFERRED TO HIM AS WAS HIS RIGHT.

"HE COULD OUTRUN ANY BEAST AND WOULD KILL DOZENS ON HIS OWN, IN LESS TIME THAN THE COMBINED PACK COULD BRING DOWN A SINGLE LAMED CALF."

THE PACK GREW STRONG THAT
UMMER. WE NEVER ATE SO WELL
AS WHEN HE WAS AMONG US.
WE'VE NEVER *ENJOYED* SUCH ENDLESS BOUNTY!
DON'T GET USED TO IT. I CAN'T STAY.

"THEN A TERRIFYING DAY. ALL OF THE WINDS WERE CONFOUNDED, CONSTANTLY CHANGING AND BLOWING TOO STRONG TO CARRY READABLE SCENTS.
WHEN WILL IT STOP, FATHER?
I DON'T KNOW.
PERHAPS THE GOD OF WOLVES CAN CALM THEM?

"WHEN THE EVIL WINDS FINALLY DIED, WE EMERGED FROM OUR DENS TO DISCOVER THE GOD OF WOLVES HAD LEFT US, WITH NO SURVIVING TRACE TO SHOW US WHERE HE WENT."

HE NEVER RETURNED.
IT WAS YOUR GOD OF WOLVES WHO CREATED THE SORCERY WINDS-- TO COVER THE MANNER AND DIRECTION OF HIS DEPARTURE.

NEXT: WHEN WE ALL LIVED IN THE FORES

WOLVES PART 2 OF 2

IN WHICH MOWGLI DOES HIS TARZAN B
MEETS YET MORE WOLVES, VISITS A CA
IN THE WILD AND DISCOVERS SOMETHI
SURPRISING THERE.

I REACHED ALASKA IN THE MIDDLE OF THE SUMMER.

I'M *STILL* NOT SURE THIS IS A GOOD IDEA, MISTER...

I'M SORRY, I'VE SPACED YOUR NAME AGAIN.

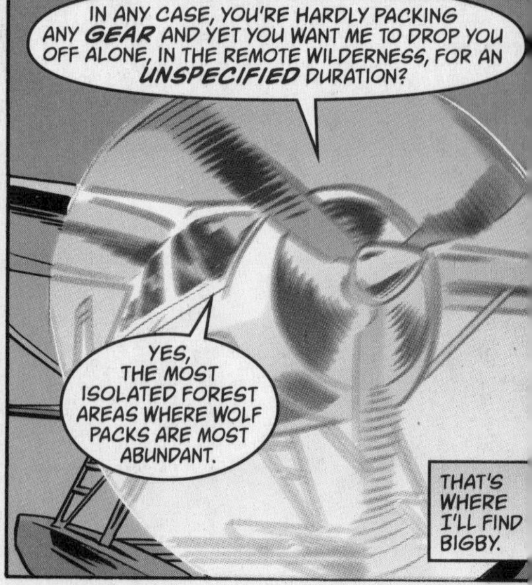

WHY? ARE YOU ANOTHER NATURALIST STUDYING THE WOLVES?
NOT ME, MR. GORDON. I'M JUST A HIGHLY IDIOSYNCRATIC TOURIST.
A SUICIDAL ONE, YOU MEAN. YOU'RE NOT PACKING NEARLY ENOUGH FOOD.
I'M SKILLED AT LIVING OFF THE LAND-- ANY LAND.

OKAY, I TRIED.
I WOULDN'T LIVE HERE DOING WHAT I DO IF I DIDN'T BELIEVE A MAN HAS A BASIC RIGHT TO DO STUPID THINGS WITH HIS OWN LIFE.
BUCKLE UP. WE GOT SOME CHOP ON THE LAKE, SO OUR LANDING WILL BE BUMPY.

IT'S SURPRISING HOW A PLACE THAT'S SO COLD IN DECEMBER CAN BE SO HOT IN JULY.

ALASKA AT THE HEIGHT OF SUMMER CAN BE AS HOT, DANK AND BUG CRAZY AS MY NATIVE INDIAN JUNGLES--WELL, NEARLY.
TRANSATLANTIC

I CACHE WHAT LITTLE GEAR I HAVE. I ONLY BROUGHT AS MUCH AS I DID TO KEEP THE NERVOUS BUSH PILOT FROM REFUSING TO TAKE ME OUT HERE ALTOGETHER.

IT'S SELDOM I GET THE CHANCE TO LIVE WILD IN THE FOREST AGAIN AS I DID IN MY YOUTH.
IT'S GLORIOUS.

I HUNT FOR MY SUPPER IN THE OLD WAY.

AND SLEEP UNDER THE GIANT TREES OF THIS UNTOUCHED WILDERNESS.

FABLETOWN'S FARM, IN UPSTATE NEW YORK.
MR. NORTH, MAY I SPEAK TO YOU FOR A MOMENT?

OF COURSE, SNOW. AND HOW OFTEN DO I HAVE TO REMIND YOU, YOU DON'T NEED TO BE SO FORMAL. WE'RE FAMILY.
NOT QUITE. YOU'RE BIGBY'S FATHER AND MY CHILDREN'S GRANDFATHER, BUT WE'RE NOT RELATED.
AND THAT'S WHAT I WANT TO TALK TO YOU ABOUT.

I NEED TO BE IN CHARGE OF MY OWN CHILDREN. I'D PREFER IT IF YOU'D STOP ENCOURAGING THEM TO SHAPE-CHANGE SO FRIVOLOUSLY.
WHY? THAT'S WHAT YOU ASKED ME TO TEACH THEM.
YES, BUT NOW THEY NEED TO SHOW US THEY CAN STAY IN HUMAN SHAPE LONG ENOUGH TO BE ABLE TO LEAVE THE FARM SOMEDAY.

THE ENDLESS RULES AND RESTRICTIONS OF THIS PLACE CONFOUND ME TO NO END.
YOU SHOULD ALL MOVE TO MY CASTLE IN THE HOMELANDS WHERE WE CAN LIVE AS FREE AS WE LIKE.
I DON'T THINK--

HOLD ON. CAN YOU FEEL THAT?
WHAT?
THE WINDS ARE CHANGING.

BUT YOU'RE THE WIND.
EXACTLY.

ON MY THIRD DAY HUNTING THROUGH THE ALASKAN FORESTS I REALIZE I'M NOT ALONE.

THEY FLANK ME ON ALL SIDES, KEEPING SILENT PACE WITH ME, JUST OUT OF SIGHT.

AND SUDDENLY I'M REMINDED THIS IS NO VACATION TRIP.
HO, BROTHERS, I AM MOWGLI OF THE SEEONEE WOLF PACK.

I'VE BEEN SEARCHING FOR YOU, IN HOPES YOU CAN HELP ME HUNT A--
SILENCE, MAN. YOU MAY SQUEAK AN APPROXIMATION OF OUR TONGUE, BUT YOU ARE NOT OF US.

SHOW ME MORE RESPECT, BROTHER WOLF!
OR I'LL HAVE TO EARN MY WAY INTO YOUR COMPANY IN THE STANDARD BLOODY WAY.

SILLY MAN. OUR LAWS DON'T APPLY TO OTHER CREATURES. NOTHING YOU CAN DO WILL MAKE YOU ONE OF US.
NOT TRUE, BROTHER. HE'S ABOUT TO JOIN EACH OF US--AS TASTY FOOD IN OUR BELLIES.
WELL SAID. THE PALE THING WILL INDEED BECOME A WOLF-- MANY WOLVES IN FACT-- FOR EXACTLY AS LONG AS IT TAKES US TO SHIT HIM OUT AGAIN.

HOLD, BROTHERS. DON'T ATTACK THIS THING.
THE WINDS HAVE CHANGED.

MASTER WANTS THE MAN BROUGHT TO HIM.

MEANWHILE, BACK AT THE FARM...
THERE'S NOTHING TO DO.

WE COULD GO DOWN TO THE SWIMMING HOLE.
IT'S TOO FAR, IF WE HAVE TO *WALK* ALL THE WAY.
ON JUST TWO SMALL, STUPID HUMAN LEGS.

STUPID NEW RULES. NO FLYING. NO CHANGING INTO ANYTHING FUN.
ONLY FOR A MONTH.
BUT THAT'S *FOREVER!* IT'S A WHOLE BUNCH OF DAYS AND A WHOLE BUNCH OF NIGHTS AND A WHOLE BUNCH OF WEEKS!

WE COULD CHANGE AFTER WE GOT OUT OF SIGHT OF THE BUILDINGS.
NO. SOMEONE WILL CATCH US. SOMEONE *ALWAYS* CATCHES US.
EVERY ANIMAL AND TROLL AND GOAT AND BIRD ON THE FARM IS A GREAT BIG STINKY *TATTLE-TALE!*

THERE'S NOTHING TO DO.

FOR TWO DAYS THE PACK LEADS ME EVER DEEPER INTO THE WOODS, SETTING A BRISK PACE THAT TESTS MY ENDURANCE.
THE LEADER OF YOUR PACK TALKS TO YOU THROUGH THE WINDS?
NO, I AM THE PACK LEADER.
BUT THE GREAT LORD OF WOLVES COMMANDS EVERY PACK IN THIS VAST LAND--AS IS HIS RIGHT.

I'VE LET MYSELF GROW SOFT, LIVING TOO LONG AMONG MEN.
IT'S HE WHO SENDS THE WINDS TO SUMMON YOU.
I SEE.

EARLY THE NEXT MORNING WE CAME UPON THE CABIN, AS FAR OUT IN THE MIDDLE OF NOWHERE AS ANYONE COULD HOPE FOR.
YOU HAVE TO GO ON ALONE FROM HERE, MOWGLI. WE'RE ALLOWED NO CLOSER THAN THIS TO THE DEN MADE OF DEAD TREES.
SURELY NOW THE GREAT AND TERRIBLE LORD WILL PUNISH YOU FOR PRETENDING KINSHIP TO WOLVES.

AFTER MORE THAN A YEAR OF SEARCHING, FALSE LEADS AND PURPOSEFUL MISDIRECTION, I SHOULDN'T GET MY HOPES UP.

BUT SOMETHING INSIDE ME KNOWS MY QUEST IS AT AN END.
HELLO?

I CAN SMELL HIM IN THIS PLACE. EVEN IF HE ISN'T HERE NOW, HE'D BEEN HERE RECENTLY AND OFTEN.
BIGBY?

OTHER STRONG SCENTS INFUSE THE CABIN TOO--WHISKEY BEING THE MOST PREVALENT.
ANYONE HOME?

I HEARD YOU, JUNGLE BOY.
HELL, I HEARD YOU FROM WAY UP ON THE *RIDGE*. I THOUGHT YOU WERE SUPPOSED TO BE *STEALTHY*.
BIGBY!
COME ON IN, MOWG. MAKE YOURSELF AT HOME.
GLEN MUNDY
CHIPS

SIT DOWN, KID. TAKE A LOAD OFF.
SO IS THIS A BUSINESS CALL, OR DID YOU JUST DROP BY TO BE *SOCIABLE?*
UHM...
GLEN MUNDY

I'VE BEEN LOOKING FOR YOU, BUT YOU LEFT A TOUGH TRAIL TO FOLLOW.
INTENTIONALLY. YOU WERE SUPPOSED TO GET THE HINT THAT I WANT TO BE LEFT ALONE.

WANT A SNORT TO TAKE THE EDGE OFF?
OR IF YOU'RE PARTICULAR ABOUT HOW YOU TAKE YOUR BOOZE, YOU CAN USE THE CUP AND I'LL DRINK FROM THE BOTTLE. NO DIFFERENCE TO ME.
NO, I'M FINE.

MORE FOR ME, THEN.
ISN'T IT A BIT TOO EARLY IN THE DAY?

NONSENSE. ANYTHING WORTH DOING IS WORTH OVERDOING.

NOW, DID YOU DROP BY SIMPLY TO QUESTION MY DRINKING HABITS, OR IS THERE SOMETHING ON YOUR MIND THAT'S ACTUALLY ANY OF YOUR DAMNED BUSINESS?
GLEN MUNDY
FABLETOWN NEEDS YOU BACK, BIGBY.

GLEN MUNDY
MALT SCOTCH WHISKY
TOO BAD. I'M ALL DONE WITH THAT.
I HAD THE WOLVES LET YOU COME THROUGH BECAUSE IT'S PART OF YOUR JOB AS ONE OF THE TOURISTS TO CHECK UP ON FABLES LIVING OUTSIDE THE COMMUNITY.

BUT, AS YOU CAN SEE, I'M BREAKING NO RULES. SO NOW THAT YOU'VE HAD YOUR LOOK, YOU CAN BE ON YOUR WAY.
NOT YET.

FEELING SUICIDAL, BOY?
OF COURSE NOT. BUT I'M HONOR BOUND TO RESCUE MY BROTHER BAGHEERA FROM JAIL.
AND THE ONLY WAY TO DO THAT IS TO BRING YOU HOME.

HERE'S A MESSAGE FROM PRINCE CHARMING.
HE'S FOUND A WAY THAT YOU AND SNOW AND YOUR CUBS CAN LIVE TOGETHER WITHOUT VIOLATING ANY FABLE-TOWN LAWS.

HOW'S THAT POSSIBLE? I'M NOT ALLOWED--
UH-OH.
GLEN MUNDY

WHAT?
SOMEONE'S HOME EARLY FROM HER FAMILY VISIT.
MOWGLI, SAY HELLO TO MY CURRENT BETTER HALF.

LOOK, DEAR, WE'VE GOT COMPANY. SARAH TANARAQ, MEET AN OLD FRIEND OF MINE, UH...
VINCENT JAGATBEHARI.
PLEASED TO MEET YOU, VINCENT.
I APOLOGIZE IF I LOOK STARTLED, BUT WE'VE NEVER HAD GUESTS BEFORE.
AND I ALWAYS ASSUMED WHEN SOMEONE FINALLY CAME TO TAKE BIGBY AWAY FROM ME, IT WOULD BE THE WOMAN HE'S TRYING SO HARD TO FORGET.

THE FARM...
WHERE DID THIS WIND COME FROM?

IT HAPPENED AS SOON AS HE LEFT.
AS SOON AS WHO LEFT?
MR. NORTH, ALONG WITH HIS LITTLE WIND CREATURES.

HE SAID IT WAS TIME FOR HIM TO GO. HE SAID YOU KNEW.
HE MENTIONED SOMETHING EARLIER, BUT-- I DIDN'T REALIZE WHAT HE MEANT.

SIS? ARE YOU OKAY?
I'M JUST TRYING TO FIGURE OUT WHAT TO TELL THE CHILDREN. THEY *ADORE* THEIR GRANDFATHER.

THEY CAN'T KEEP HAVING THE *MEN* IN THEIR LIVES RUN OUT ON THEM.

BACK IN ALASKA...
I CAN'T GET DRUNK. BUT A STEADY WHISKEY FLOW KEEPS ME INEBRIATED JUST ENOUGH TO STAY COMFORTABLY NUMB, FOR THE MOST PART.

SARAH DOESN'T APPROVE, OF COURSE, BUT SHE'S SMART ENOUGH TO REALIZE SHE DOESN'T HAVE MUCH SAY IN THE MATTER.
SHE HAS TO TAKE ME IN THE BROKEN CONDITION SHE FOUND ME, RIGHT?

SO HOW DID YOU FIND ME, MOWGLI?
I THOUGHT I'D COVERED MY TRACKS PRETTY WELL.
YOU DID. I DOUBT ANYONE BUT ME COULD'VE FOUND YOU. NOT TOO MANY OTHER FABLES WOULD THINK TO INTERVIEW WOLVES.

MUCH LESS HAVE THE ABILITY TO SPEAK TO THEM.
EVEN SO, YOU ALMOST LOST ME AT THE BERING STRAIT. I MADE DAMN SURE YOU DIDN'T HOP ANY PLANE OR BOAT.

SO I NATURALLY ASSUMED YOU'D DOUBLED BACK INTO RUSSIA.
THAT'S WHAT ANYONE WHO'D GOTTEN THAT FAR WAS MEANT TO THINK. RUSSIA'S PRETTY BIG, WITH LOTS OF WILDERNESS TO GET LOST IN.

BUT THE IDEA YOU'D DECIDED TO LIVE
RUSSIA JUST DIDN'T FIT. I RECALL ONCE
YOU'D MENTIONED HOW MUCH TROUBLE
YOU'D HAD TRYING TO LEARN THEIR
LANGUAGE.
YEAH, I NEVER COULD GET THE EAR FOR IT, BACK IN MY WAR DAYS.

I HAD TO REMEMBER WHO YOU WERE AND WHAT YOU COULD DO BEFORE I REALIZED HOW YOU MADE IT ACROSS THE STRAIT TO ALASKA.
YOU SWAM IT, RIGHT?

OF COURSE. IT TOOK ME A COUPLE OF DAYS LONGER
HAN I'D PLANNED WHEN A BIG STORM CAME UP. BUT
NEVER RAN OUT OF AIR AND THE COLD DOESN'T GET
O ME. SO, ALL IN ALL, IT WAS AN ENJOYABLE SWIM."

I SHOULD'VE PAID YOU MORE, BACK WHEN I WAS RUNNING THE TOURISTS. YOU'RE TOO CLEVER BY HALF.
NOT TO CHANGE THE SUBJECT, BUT HOW MUCH DOES SARAH KNOW ABOUT YOU?

SHE KNOWS I HAVE CHILDREN WITH SOME OTHER WOMAN DOWN IN THE LOWER STATES, BUT NO OTHER DETAILS.
AND NOTHING ABOUT MY TRUE NATURE.

SHE DISCOVERED BIGBY RAWLINS HAS SOME SORT OF SPECIAL *RAPPORT* WITH THE WOLF PACKS AROUND HERE, BUT SHE DOESN'T ASCRIBE ANY SUPERNATURAL POWERS TO IT.

CREDIT THAT TO THE LATEST TRENDS AMONG TREE-HUGGING IDIOT *NATURALISTS* WHO'VE DETERMINED THAT WOLVES WERE NEVER ANY DANGER TO MEN.
GOD BLESS THE BROTHERHOOD OF *ALL* CREATURES.

"SHE'S NEVER SEEN ME CHANGE FORM. I GO FAR AWAY FROM HERE WHEN I FEEL THE NEED TO SPEND SOME DAYS RUNNING THE BOOZE AND GENERAL FRUSTRATION OUT OF MY SYSTEM."

I NEED TIME TO THINK ABOUT PRINCE CHARMING'S OFFER.
AND YOUR STANDING TOURIST ORDERS DICTATE THAT YOU NEED TO TALK TO SARAH, TO MAKE SURE I HAVEN'T REVEALED ANY FABLE SECRETS TO HER.

SO WHY DON'T YOU TEND TO THAT WHILE I GO DOWN TO THE RIVER AND FETCH WATER FOR TONIGHT'S SUPPER?

I'LL START SUPPER AS SOON AS I FINISH BRUSHING DOWN LAZY BONES. HE'S HAD A LONG THREE DAYS HAULING NEW SUPPLIES UP FROM TOWN.
TAKE YOUR TIME.

SO, WILL BIGBY BE GOING WITH YOU WHEN YOU LEAVE, VINCENT?
I DON'T KNOW YET. I HOPE SO.

SORRY.
I DIDN'T MEAN TO BE CRUEL.
DON'T WORRY. YOU'RE FINE.

I ALWAYS KNEW I WAS TEMPORARY. HE'D BE OUT THE DOOR THE MOMENT SHE CROOKED HER FINGER TO TAKE HIM BACK.
THAT'S THE NATURE OF REBOUND RELATIONSHIPS, RIGHT?

MY JOB WAS TO SUPPLEMENT THE WHISKEY IN HELPING HIM TO GET OVER HER.
I WOULDN'T INTERFERE, BUT HE'S NEEDED FOR A VITAL MI--UHM, A VITAL SITUATION.

YOU WERE ABOUT TO SAY "MISSION," WEREN'T YOU? IS HE SOME KIND OF GOVERNMENT AGENT?
I'M NOT AT LIBERTY TO SAY.

I SUSPECTED SOMETHING LIKE THAT. HE'S ALWAYS TREATED ME GENTLY, BUT A BLIND *IMBECILE* COULD SENSE HOW DANGEROUS HE IS.

SO THE OTHER WOMAN HAS *NOTHING* TO DO WITH THIS?
UHM...NOT ENTIRELY.

LOVELY.
JUST *LOVELY.*

WELL, TAKE HIM AND *GO*, IF THAT'S WHAT YOU'RE HERE FOR.

READY TO GO?
SURE.
HOW'D SHE TAKE IT?
GRACEFULLY ENOUGH TO MAKE ME FEEL LIKE A SHITHEAD OF THE FIRST ORDER.

About a week later...
HERE WE ARE, LAZY BONES.

HOME AGAIN, HOME AGAIN.
STARTING OVER. NO MORE LIVING OUT WITH THE WOLVES FOR US, OLD DUFFER.

And at a small woodcarver's hut in the Homelands...
WHAT IS IT, POP?
I'M NOT SURE.

YOU LOOK WORRIED.
I THOUGHT I HEARD SOMETHING, OR MAYBE--WELL, NEVER MIND.
PROBABLY JUST A CHANGE IN THE WINDS.

LATE AT NIGHT AT THE FARM...
HELLO? IS SOME-ONE DOWN THERE?

THERE BETTER NOT BE ANY CUBS WHO SHOULD BE IN BED RAIDING THE ICEBOX.
NO, SNOW, IT'S JUST ME.

COLIN! WHY ARE YOU HERE AGAIN? IS THERE MORE TROUBLE COMING?
NO. AT LEAST I DON'T THINK SO.
THEN WHY--

IT'S HARD TO BE SURE, SNOW, BUT I THINK I'M HERE TO SAY GOODBYE. I DON'T THINK YOU NEED ME ANY-MORE.
WHY? HOW?

IF I HAD TO GUESS, IT'S BECAUSE THINGS GET BETTER NOW--FOR YOU, I MEAN.
AND FOR ME, I THINK IT'S FINALLY TIME FOR ME TO MOVE ALONG TO WHATEVER HAPPENS NEXT.
NEXT: BETTER DAYS?

CHAPTER ONE: SECRET AGENT MAN

WOW! THAT'S A--
THAT'S RIGHT, ROSE RED, IT'S A BEANSTALK-- ONE OF THE MAGIC ONES FROM JACK'S ORIGINAL MAGIC BEAN STASH.
WHICH IS WHY WE NEVER PAID MUCH ATTENTION TO JACK WHEN HE CLAIMED TO STILL HAVE SOME OF THE BEANS. HE DIDN'T KNOW WE HAD THEM ALL ALONG.

SO *THIS* IS WHAT YOU'VE BEEN UP TO OUT HERE FOR THE PAST TWO YEARS? ALL THE SECRET COMINGS AND GOINGS? WHY DIDN'T YOU *TELL* ME?
UNTIL NOW, YOU DIDN'T NEED TO KNOW.

BIGBY TAUGHT ME THAT MUCH. COMPARTMENTALIZATION IS THE BE-ALL AND END-ALL OF THE SPOOK GAME. NO ONE *GETS* TO KNOW UNLESS THEY ABSOLUTELY *NEED* TO KNOW.
BASIC OPERATIONAL DOCTRINE, KID.

BUT THIS--!
YOU CAN'T--!
IT STICKS OUT LIKE A SORE THUMB! A *GIANT* SORE THUMB! THIS IS GOING TO ATTRACT ALL KINDS OF MUNDY ATTENTION TO THE FARM!

NOT AT ALL. IT'S COMPLETELY IMAGINARY UNTIL YOU GET CLOSE ENOUGH.
NO ONE CAN SEE IT FROM A DISTANCE. A MUNDY PILOT COULD FLY WITHIN 300 *FEET* OF IT AND NEVER KNOW IT'S THERE.

AND SINCE NO FLIGHT PATHS PASS WITHIN TWENTY MILES OF THIS PLACE, WE'RE FINE.
THE BEANSTALK'S BASIC STRUCTURE IS TRANS-DIMENSIONAL.

THOUGH THE ROOTS ARE FIRMLY IN OUR WORLD, SOMEWHERE ALONG THE WAY IT ENDS UP POKING ITSELF INTO THE CLOUD KINGDOMS.
THIS IS ALL VERY INFORMATIVE, BUT CAN WE GET TO THE PRACTICAL BUSINESS?
ANSATLANT

I ASSUME I'M GOING TO CLIMB THIS THING?
EXACTLY.
WHERE'S MY GEAR?

IT'S WAITING FOR YOU UPSTAIRS, ALONG WITH YOUR SPECIFIC INSTRUCTIONS. WE THOUGHT IT BETTER THAT WAY, TO FURTHER GUARD AGAINST ANY-THING LEAKING OUT.
YOUR CONTACT WILL MEET YOU AT THE TOP.

THEN I MIGHT AS WELL GET STARTED.
ARE YOU SURE THERE ISN'T ANYTHING YOU WANT ME TO TELL SNOW?
I'M SURE, ROSE.

IF I DON'T RETURN, I WAS NEVER HERE IN THE FIRST PLACE.
IF I DO, I CAN TELL HER MYSELF.

WAKE UP, BAGHEERA, IT'S EMANCIPATION DAY FOR ALL IMPRISONED FABLES OF THE BLACK PANTHERISH PERSUASION.

REALLY? I'M FREE TO GO?
YOU'RE OFFICIALLY SPRUNG, BUDDY.
HERE'S YOUR PARDON-- SIGNED AND SEALED.

I CAN GO ANYWHERE I WANT?
ANYWHERE ON THE FARM, AT LEAST.
GET OFF ME, YOU GIANT RAT!

ANYWHERE NOT RESTRICTED, THAT IS!
WHERE'S HE OFF TO LIKE A ROCKET?
SOMEPLACE THAT DOESN'T RESEMBLE A CAGE, I IMAGINE.

SPEAKING OF WHICH, LET'S GET THIS THING DISMANTLED TODAY. IT'S BEEN A BLIGHT ON OUR TOWN SQUARE FOR ENTIRELY TOO LONG.
HE'LL PROBABLY REMEMBER TO THANK YOU, ONCE HE'S SETTLED DOWN A BIT.
I EXPECT.

CHAPTER TWO: CASTLES IN THE SKY

YES, IT'S ME, AND YOU REALLY CAN GET DOWN. IT'S SOLID FROM THE TOP, EVEN THOUGH YOU COULD PASS THROUGH FROM BELOW. THAT'S THE WAY THE ENCHANTMENT WORKS.
HONESTLY, I DON'T THINK I'VE EVER SEEN YOU AFRAID OF ANYTHING BEFORE, BIGBY.

AND YOU STILL HAVEN'T. NERVOUS ISN'T THE SAME AS SCARED.
REMEMBER, ME AND MINE DIDN'T EVOLVE FROM MONKEYS LIKE YOU AND YOURS. I DON'T HAVE CLIMBING HARD-WIRED INTO ME FROM A MILLION GENERATIONS PAST.

POINT TAKEN, BUT YOU REALLY CAN STEP DOWN. SEE? I'M JUMPING UP AND DOWN RIGHT NEXT TO YOU AND I'M NOT FALLING THROUGH.
TRUST ME. I'VE BEEN LIVING UP HERE FOR MONTHS, PREPARING THE WAY FOR YOU WITH THE LOCALS.

THERE'S REALLY NO NEED TO BE SCARED.
NERVOUS.
RIGHT. NERVOUS. THAT'S WHAT I SAID.

OKAY, HERE GOES NOTHING.
IF YOU DO FALL THROUGH, YOU'LL HAVE A LONG TIME TO REGRET LISTENING TO ME ON THE WAY DOWN.

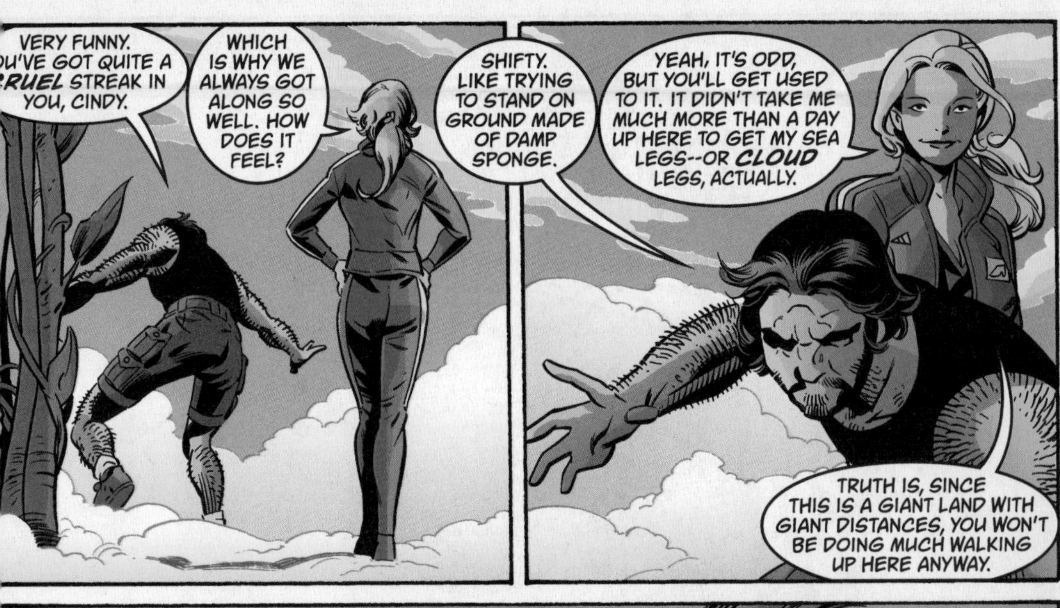
VERY FUNNY. YOU'VE GOT QUITE A CRUEL STREAK IN YOU, CINDY.
WHICH IS WHY WE ALWAYS GOT ALONG SO WELL. HOW DOES IT FEEL?
SHIFTY. LIKE TRYING TO STAND ON GROUND MADE OF DAMP SPONGE.
YEAH, IT'S ODD, BUT YOU'LL GET USED TO IT. IT DIDN'T TAKE ME MUCH MORE THAN A DAY UP HERE TO GET MY SEA LEGS--OR CLOUD LEGS, ACTUALLY.
TRUTH IS, SINCE THIS IS A GIANT LAND WITH GIANT DISTANCES, YOU WON'T BE DOING MUCH WALKING UP HERE ANYWAY.

RADISKOP!
YES, CINDERELLA?
CAN YOU INFORM OUR HOST THAT THE GUEST OF HONOR HAS ARRIVED?
YOU BETCHA!

HE SEEMS ENTHUSIASTIC.
RADY'S A BIG SWEETHEART.
BIG IS RIGHT--BIG ENOUGH TO SWALLOW US BOTH IN TWO OR THREE BITES.

HELP ME BREAK CAMP WHILE WE WAIT FOR OUR TRANSPORT TO ARRIVE.
WE WON'T BE COMING BACK THIS WAY.

LESS THAN AN HOUR LATER...
YOUNG HUMBERJON IS TAKING US TO THE WIZARD ULMORE'S CASTLE. THAT'S OUR STAGING AREA FOR THE MISSION.
NICE VIEW.

Extreme care should be taken not to do or say anything that might jeopardize the new and fragile diplomatic relations between Fabletown and the Cloud Kingdoms.

EVEN THOUGH THE CLOUD KINGDOMS EXIST IN THEIR OWN DIMENSION, IN A SEEMINGLY PARADOXICAL WAY THEY ALSO EXIST IN THE SKY OVER EVERY KNOWN WORLD.

THAT'S KEPT US SAFE SO FAR FROM THE ADVERSARY'S ARMIES.
BUT THE DIMENSIONAL DOORWAYS ARE ALWAYS OPEN GOING IN THE OTHER DIRECTION.

THREE DAYS LATER...
WE SHOULDN'T NEED ANYTHING BUT GRAVITY TO DO THE TRICK.
ARE YOU READY TO GO, BIGBY? GOT ALL YOUR EQUIPMENT?
THE HOLE'S DUG, SIR.

I ALMOST SLIPPED THROUGH IT MYSELF.
I HOPE SO. THERE'S NO ROOM FOR ANYTHING ELSE.

BETTER HOLD YOUR HAND DIRECTLY OVER THE HOLE, ULMORE. I CAN'T JUMP VERY FAR UNDER ALL THIS WEIGHT.
BE CARELESS DOWN THERE!

Stage Two:
Insertion.
You will parachute
into the Empire
district of Calabri
Anagni.

Be sure to
pick a
wilderness
location for
your drop
zone.

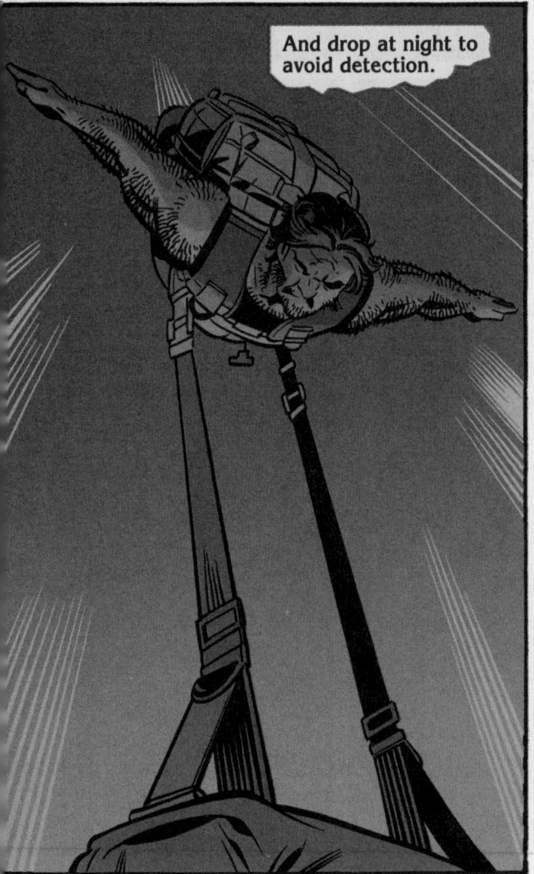
And drop at night to
avoid detection.

CHAPTER THREE: BEHIND ENEMY LINES

Pick a landing site close enough to your target to be within a day's travel, making sure you stay far away from the Imperial City.

Plant your extraction bean in some remote location. Take note that it will take approximately twelve hours to fully deploy.

Travel only at night.

Avoid all enemy contact.

If you arrive at the target site during daylight hours, wait until late the next night to begin operations.

Stage Three: Preliminary Objectives.
First remove all guards from the area.

CKRICCK

It's vital that you kill swiftly and silently...

...so that no alarm can be raised in the woodcarver's cabin.

DEVIL SPAWN!

WHAT'S THIS?
DIRE SORCERY!
NOT AT *ALL*, GENTLEMEN.

IT'S JUST MY SON, GUARDING MY BACK.
YOU CAN DROP THEM NOW, BOY. I'M *READY* FOR THEM.

Next enter the grove of magic trees and prepare them with the Special Packages—spaced for maximum effect.

Stage Four: Primary Objectives.
When the grove is prepared, you can enter the wood-carver's hut.
IF THE OCEAN WERE WHISKEY AND I WAS A DUCK...

...I'D DIVE TO THE BOTTOM AND DRINK IT ALL UP!

B-BE VERY QUIET NOW, PIN-HIC-PINOCCHIO.

SHHHHHHH, MR. WOODY OWL. IT'S VERY IMPORTANT WE DON'T WAKE MY DA--MY DA--DON'T WAKE THE EVIL, BLOODY-HANDED ADVERSARY.

If possible, try to free the Blue Fairy from her imprisonment. If that fails, try to destroy her.
KINDLY OLD CONQUERORS NEED THEIR SLEEP.

BIGBY?
SHHHHHHH, PINOCCHIO. GEPPETTO'S SLEEPING ONLY TWO ROOMS AWAY, AND WE DON'T WANT TO WAKE HIM.

WHAT ARE YOU DOING HERE, BIGBY?
TRYING TO MURDER YOUR DAD'S POWER SOURCE. DIDN'T WORK, THOUGH.

THE SPELLS PROTECTING HER ARE NEARLY AS COMPLEX AS THOSE PROTECTING MY DAD.
THE VERY SAME CONCLUSION I CAME TO ABOUT TWENTY SECONDS AGO.

Only if an opportunity presents itself, without jeopardizing the main mission, attempt to recruit Pinocchio into returning with you to Fabletown.
I ALSO CAME TO GET YOU, IF YOU'RE READY TO COME HOME NOW.

Our sorcerer's best theory is that his second transformation to flesh probably included the same loyalty bonds that infect all new puppet creations.
HOW CAN I DO THAT, BIGBY?

MY GOODNESS.
WHAT'S GOING ON HERE?
GEPPETTO!
OH, NO!

CHAPTER FOUR: THE ISRAEL ANALOGY

EVER HEAR OF A COUNTRY CALLED ISRAEL?
WHO KNOWS? MAYBE. WHY'S THAT IMPORTANT?

HERE'S WHAT YOU NEED TO KNOW ABOUT IT.
ISRAEL IS A TINY COUNTRY SURROUNDED BY MUCH LARGER COUNTRIES DEDICATED TO ITS EVENTUAL TOTAL DESTRUCTION.
AND WHY SHOULD THAT CONCERN ME?

BECAUSE THEY STAY ALIVE BY BEING A BUNCH OF TOUGH LITTLE BASTARDS WHO MAKE THE OTHER GUYS PAY DEARLY EVERY TIME THEY DO ANYTHING AGAINST ISRAEL.
SOME IN THE WIDER WORLD CONSTANTLY WAIL AND MOAN ABOUT THE ENDLESS CYCLE OF VIOLENCE AND REPRISAL.

BUT SINCE THE ALTERNATIVE IS NON-EXISTENCE, THE ISRAELIS SEEM DETERMINED TO KEEP AT IT.
THEY HAVE A LOT OF GRIT AND IRON. I'M A BIG FAN OF THEM.

ARE YOU NEAR TO BEING DONE? I'D LIKE TO GO BACK TO SLEEP.
HERE'S THE PART THAT CONCERNS YOU. FABLETOWN HAS DECIDED TO ADOPT THE ISRAEL TEMPLATE IN WHOLE.
YOU'VE NO DOUBT GUESSED THAT YOU GUYS PLAY THE PART OF THE VAST POWERS ARRAYED AGAINST US.

EVERY TIME YOU HURT US WE'RE GOING TO DAMAGE YOU MUCH *WORSE* IN RETURN.
IT WILL ALWAYS HAPPEN. ALWAYS. YOU'RE THE ONLY ONE WHO CAN END THE CYCLE.

AND KEEP THIS IN MIND. YOU HAVE A HUGE *EMPIRE* TO PROTECT.
GUARD THE TEN MILLION MOST LIKELY TARGETS AND THERE WILL *STILL* BE A HUNDRED MILLION RIPE, UNPROTECTED TARGETS WE CAN HIT.

OKAY, I UNDERSTAND NOW. I'LL *PONDER* YOUR THREAT.
NOT SO FAST, OLD GAFFER. ACCOUNTS AREN'T *BALANCED* YET.
YOU STILL HAVE THE WOODEN SOLDIER RAID AGAINST FABLETOWN TO PAY FOR.

BUT YOU ALREADY KNOW YOU CAN'T HURT US.
THINK SO? I'M ABOUT TO *STICK* IT TO YOU WHERE IT HURTS MOST. SEE THIS? IT'S MUNDY MAGIC, WHICH THEY CALL HIGH-TECH. IT'S A RADIO TRANSMITTER.

IT'S ABOUT TO TALK TO ANOTHER BUNCH OF MUNDY MAGIC CALLED PLASTIC *EXPLOSIVE,* FORMED INTO ABOUT THREE DOZEN BOMBS STRAPPED TO TREE TRUNKS.
THIS WOULD BE A GOOD TIME TO *DUCK,* BECAUSE WHEN I PUSH THIS LITTLE RED BUTTON--

SOMETIME LATER...
COME ON, OLD MAN. YOUR CABIN'S STARTED TO BURN.

AND EVEN IF THOSE SPELLS PROTECT YOU FROM BURNING UP WITH IT, I DOUBT YOU'LL WANT TO WAIT FOR THEM TO FIND YOU TWO UNDER THE SCORCHED REMAINS.
COUGH-COUGH!

I'VE JUST TAKEN YOUR MAGIC GROVE AWAY FROM YOU.
YEAH, I KNOW IT'LL GROW BACK--EVENTUALLY--BUT I SUSPECT IT'LL BE AT LEAST A GENERATION BEFORE YOU CAN PRODUCE NEW WOODEN CHILDREN FROM IT.

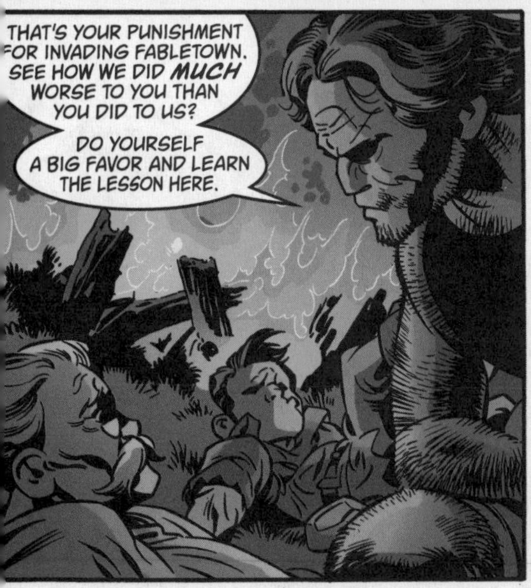
THAT'S YOUR PUNISHMENT FOR INVADING FABLETOWN. SEE HOW WE DID MUCH WORSE TO YOU THAN YOU DID TO US?
DO YOURSELF A BIG FAVOR AND LEARN THE LESSON HERE.

THAT WAS THE STICK, NOW HERE'S THE CARROT. MOST OF THE HEADS FROM YOUR INVASION FORCE ARE STILL ALIVE.
WE MIGHT BE WILLING TO EXCHANGE THEM FOR THINGS WE WANT--IF YOU CAN CONVINCE US YOU'RE INCLINED TO BE NICE FROM NOW ON.

Stage Five: Extraction.
After completion of all objectives, return to the extraction point as quickly as possible, no matter the time of day.

The beanstalk should have fully deployed by the time you reach it. Plant the remaining bombs at its base in places of concealment...

...to avoid detection from any forces that might give chase.

CLIMB FASTER, YOU FILTHY GOBS, OR THE EMPEROR WILL KILL EVERY BLOODY ONE OF YOU!

Be sure to activate the radio detonator while still in the Empire dimension to ensure a good signal.

IMPERIAL APPROVED GODS AND DEMONS SAVE US!

Your final ascent will be up the secondary escape line.

Don't forget to grab it before destroying the beanstalk.

End of mission briefing. Good luck and be careful, Bigby.

CHAPTER FIVE: HOME IS THE HUNTER

I JUST FINISHED READING YOUR AFTER-ACTION REPORT AND IT'S ***MARVELOUS!*** ONE HUNDRED PERCENT SUCCESS!

I HATE TO ADMIT IT, MR. MAYOR, BUT YOU CRAFTED A GOOD PLAN.

WELL DONE, SHERIFF!

NOT MY NAME ANYMORE, BEAST. THAT'S ***YOUR*** HEADACHE FROM NOW ON.

SO YOU AREN'T COMING BACK TO YOUR OLD JOB?

NOPE. I'M RETIRED.
FOR GOOD.
AH, YES-- WELL, PERHAPS IT'S TIME WE DISCUSSED THE DETAILS OF THE RETIREMENT PACKAGE I PROMISED.

I CAN'T BELIEVE YOU'RE REALLY HERE, BIGBY!
WOAH!

UHM... NICE TO SEE YOU TOO, FLY.
UH, YEAH... I GUESS WHAT I MEANT TO SAY WAS...UHM, I REALLY MISSED YOU AND WELCOME HOME.

SENTIMENTS WE ALL SHARE, FLYCATCHER.
NOW, IF YOU'LL EXCUSE US, BIGBY AND I HAVE A BIT OF PRIVATE BUSINESS TO RESOLVE.

SEVERAL DAYS LATER, AT FABLETOWN'S FARM ANNEX IN UPSTATE NEW YORK...

OKAY, WILL YOU PLEASE TELL ME NOW WHERE WE'RE GOING?
I DON'T UNDERSTAND WHAT THE BIG SECRET'S ALL ABOUT.

RELAX, SISTER. IT'S A SURPRISE.
AND WE'RE HERE. AT LEAST WE'RE AS FAR AS WE CAN GET BY TRUCK.

WE WALK FROM HERE--OR, TO BE MORE PRECISE, YOU DO.
I WISH YOU'D DRESSED BETTER, SNOW.
SORRY, BUT WHEN I CHOSE MY ENSEMBLE THIS MORNING--
--I DIDN'T REALIZE YOU'D BE KIDNAPPING ME FOR A WILDERNESS ADVENTURE.

AND WHAT DO YOU MEAN? I WALK ALONE FROM HERE?
HEAD THAT WAY, SIS. I'LL BE WAITING HERE WHEN YOU'RE READY TO COME BACK.

CHAPTER SIX: RESTORATION

BIGBY!

HELLO, SNOW.
YOU CAME BACK! YOU'RE HERE! YOU--!

OH, NO! YOU'RE NOT ALLOWED TO--
YOU HAVE TO GO! RIGHT NOW!
IF THEY CATCH YOU ON THE FARM THEY'LL KILL YOU!

SETTLE DOWN, SNOW. YOU'RE BABBLING.
BUT--
I KNOW I'M NOT ALLOWED ON THE FARM, BUT THIS ISN'T THE FARM.

OF COURSE IT IS!
NOT ANY LONGER. FROM NOW ON, THE FAR
ENDS WHERE ROS
RED DROPPED YOU OFF.
THIS AREA BELONGS TO ME NOW-- OR US, IF YOU LIKE.

I DON'T UNDERSTAND.
I BOUGHT THIS LAND FROM FABLETOWN, IN RETURN FOR ENDING A WAR--OR MAYBE *STARTING* ONE. I GUESS WE'LL SEE.
COME ON. TAKE A WALK WITH ME. I WANT TO SHOW YOU A THING OR TWO.

WAIT!
THERE'S SOMETHING I NEED TO--
BIGBY, DID OUR *SON* FIND YOU?

OF COURSE.
GHOST, GIVE YOUR MOTHER A KISS.

!
WUFF

MOMMY'S CRYING. WHY'S SHE CRYING, DADDY? DID I UPSET HER AGAIN?
DON'T WORRY, SON. THOSE ARE HAPPY TEARS, NOT SAD ONES.

YOU NAMED HIM GHOST?
SEEMED TO FIT.

HE'LL BE SAFE HERE. HE'S LEARNED HOW TO KEEP HIS EXISTENCE SECRET. YOU AND I ARE THE ONLY LIVING CREATURES WHO KNOW ABOUT HIM.
WE'LL HAVE TO DECIDE WHEN TO INTRODUCE HIM TO HIS BROTHERS AND SISTERS.

SO NOW, LIKE I SAID, LET'S THE THREE OF US GO FOR A WALK.
HOLD ON, I NEED TO GO BACK AND GET MY CANE.

NO, YOU WON'T NEED IT.
YOU CAN LEAN ON ME FROM NOW ON.

CHAPTER SEVEN: THE BIG VALLEY

OKAY, THAT'S A CONVERSATION WE NEED TO HAVE REAL SOON.
BUT FIRST THINGS FIRST.

SINCE THERE ARE SO MANY NATURAL CAVES IN THESE HILLS, I DECIDED TO USE ONE TO KEEP CERTAIN THINGS HIDDEN.

YOU HAVE SOME WORK TO DO BEFORE I CAN LET YOU SEE THE KIDS--OUR OTHER KIDS.
FIRST SOME READING. THIS BOX IS FULL OF ALL THE LETTERS THEY WROTE YOU. EACH ONE HAS A COPY OF YOUR REPLY PAPER-CLIPPED TO IT.
LETTERS
GIFTS
PHOTOS

THEN YOU CAN UNWRAP ALL THE GIFTS THEY SENT YOU FOR CHRISTMAS, BIRTHDAYS, AND FATHER'S DAY.
MAKE DAMN SURE YOU MEMORIZE WHO GAVE YOU WHAT.

AND FINALLY WE'LL GO OVER THE GIFTS YOU SENT THEM, SO IT DOESN'T COME AS A COMPLETE SURPRISE TO YOU WHEN THEY MENTION THEM.
GOT IT.

LATER...
WE CAN TALK ABOUT HER IN DETAIL IF YOU LIKE, BUT THE GIST IS THIS.
SARAH'S ONE OF THE WAYS I TRIED TO FORGET YOU. I ALSO TRIED BOOZE AND SOLITUDE.
NOTHING WORKED. HOW COULD IT?

SO HERE IT IS, ONE LAST TIME AND THEN I'LL LEAVE YOU ALONE FOREVER, IF THAT'S WHAT YOU DECIDE.
I LOVE YOU, SNOW, AND HAVE SINCE THE HOUR WE FIRST MET.

HELL, I WANTED YOU EVEN BEFORE THEN. SINCE BEFORE WE EXISTED.
AS IF EVERY MOVEMENT OF EVERY STAR AND PLANET, EVERY TICK OF CREATION'S CLOCK OCCURRED ONLY SO THAT WE COULD SOMEDAY FIND EACH OTHER.
BIGBY, I--

I'M CERTAINLY NO HANDSOME PRINCE, COME TO STEAL YOU AWAY FROM ALL THE CARES OF THE WORLD. I CAN NEVER OFFER YOU RICHES AND PALACES OR ANY SORT OF LUXURY.
BUT I THINK YOU'VE HAD YOUR FILL OF SUCH THINGS BY NOW.

WHAT I CAN OFFER YOU IS A HOME IN OUR VALLEY, WHERE WE CAN RAISE OUR KIDS.
AND I'M OLD-FASHIONED ENOUGH THAT I THINK WE SHOULD BE MARRIED TO DO IT.

I THINK THAT'S YOUR CUE TO SAY SOMETHING NOW.

OKAY.
YOU'VE DEFEATED ME.

YOU WIN.

CHAPTER EIGHT: THE WEDDING

DAYS SEEMED TO BLUR TOGETHER.

HOW CAN EVERY SINGLE ONE OF YOU RUFFIANS POSSIBLY BE SHY ALL OF A SUDDEN? YOU'VE SEEN HIS PICTURES AND READ HIS LETTERS.

COME AND MEET YOUR FATHER.

PLANS WERE MADE.
WHAT I HAVE TO SAY IS SIMPLY THIS.
IF YOU PICK ANYONE ELSE AS YOUR MAID OF HONOR, FORGET FREE BABYSITTING FOREVER.

REYNARD! FINALLY! WHERE ARE THE TROLLS?
RELAX, BOY BLUE. THEY'RE ON THE WAY. THEY DON'T MOVE AS FAST AS I DO. BUT THEY'RE STURDY. EACH ONE CAN PACK A TON.

GOOD, BECAUSE THIS IS AS FAR AS THE TRUCKS WILL GO, AND WE NEED TO GET ALL OF THIS HEAVY STUFF OVER THOSE HILLS.
I'VE PUT UP NOTICES FOR EVERY CARPENTER, PLUMBER, BRICK-LAYER AND STONE MASON IN FABLE-TOWN.

GET THEM ALL OUT HERE BY YESTERDAY, FLY.
I'M DETERMINED TO HAVE THEIR HOUSE FINISHED BY THE TIME THEY GET BACK FROM THEIR HONEY-MOON.

I'M IN THE AIR NOW, MAYBE SIX HOURS OUT. WHATEVER YOU DO, DON'T LET THEM START WITHOUT ME!

THINGS GOT HECTIC, AS THINGS WILL.
THE NORTH WIND? MY FATHER WAS LIVING AT THE FARM? RAISING MY KIDS?
AND THEY'RE AFRAID OF LETTING ME OUT THERE? DON'T THEY RECOGNIZE A REAL MONSTER WHEN THEY SEE ONE?

SO THE WOLF AND THE PRINCESS AND ALL SEVEN CHILDREN WILL LIVE OUT IN THE WOODS?
SIX KIDS, FRAU TOTENKINDER, NOT SEVEN.
OH YES, SIX. AT MY AGE IT'S SO HARD TO REMEMBER THINGS.

SO JUST LIKE THAT, BIGBY AND SNOW GET AN ENTIRE VALLEY ALL TO THEMSELVES?
THEY EARNED IT. WHEN YOU'VE SERVED FABLETOWN FOR A FEW CENTURIES, WE'LL WORRY ABOUT WHAT YOU'VE EARNED.

PRIME RIB! PORK ROASTS! SUCH A FEAST I'M GOING TO PREPARE FOR YOU!
AND A WEDDING CAKE TWENTY LAYERS HIGH!
A THOUSAND CANDLES IS MY GIFT, TO MATCH THE STARS WE DINE UNDER!
CAKES

HAVE I ARRIVED IN TIME, GRIMBLE? AM I TOO LATE?
FOR WHAT?
HEY, DID YOU KNOW THERE'S A BIG WEDDING DAY AFTER TOMORROW?

AND PLEASE DON'T BE FRIGHTENED WHEN YOU SEE BIGBY WOLF. HE'S REALLY A NICE GUY NOW. HONEST.
WHY WOULD I BE FRIGHTENED OF A MAN I'VE NEVER MET BEFORE?

I'LL NEVER FORGIVE YOU, PRINCE CHARMING.
WHAT? DID I DO SOMETHING TO YOU?
IT'S WHAT YOU DIDN'T DO. YOU DIDN'T KEEP YOUR PROMISE TO PROVIDE ALL THE ANIMAL FARM FABLES WITH PERMANENT TRANS-FORMATIONS.

IF YOU HAD, I COULD HAVE BECOME A MAN, LIKE BIGBY DID. AND I WOULD'VE HAD MORE THAN ENOUGH TIME TO WIN SNOW WHILE HE WAS AWAY.
WHO ARE YOU AGAIN? DO WE EVEN KNOW EACH OTHER?

AM I DOING THE RIGHT THING?

AM I ABOUT TO MAKE A BIG MISTAKE?

DEARLY BELOVED.
WE ARE GATHERED HERE TOGETHER, IN THE SIGHT OF GOD, TO JOIN THIS MAN AND THIS WOMAN TOGETHER IN HOLY MATRIMONY.

WHICH IS AN HONORABLE ESTATE, INSTITUTED BY GOD IN HEAVEN, INTO WHICH THESE TWO PRESENT COME NOW TO BE JOINED.
WARNING:
YOU ARE LEAVING FARM TERRITORY

THEREFORE, IF ANY FABLE CAN SHOW *JUST* CAUSE WHY THEY MAY NOT LAWFULLY BE JOINED TOGETHER, LET HIM SPEAK NOW OR ELSE HEREAFTER HOLD HIS PEACE.

WILT THOU, BIGBY WOLF, HAVE THIS WOMAN TO BE THY WEDDED WIFE, TO LIVE TOGETHER AFTER GOD'S ORDINANCE IN THE HOLY STATE OF MATRIMONY?
WILT THOU LOVE HER, COMFORT HER, HONOR AND KEEP HER, IN SICKNESS AND IN HEALTH, FORSAKING ALL OTHERS, AND KEEP THEE ONLY UNTO HER, SO LONG AS YOU BOTH SHALL LIVE?
YES-- I MEAN, *I WILL.*

WILT THOU, SNOW WHITE, HAVE THIS MAN TO BE THY WEDDED HUSBAND, TO LIVE TOGETHER AFTER GOD'S ORDINANCE IN THE HOLY STATE OF MATRIMONY?
WILT THOU OBEY HIM AND SERVE HIM, LOVE, HONOR AND KEEP HIM IN SICKNESS AND IN HEALTH, AND FORSAKING ALL OTHERS, KEEP THEE ONLY UNTO HIM SO LONG AS YOU BOTH SHALL LIVE?
I WILL.

I TAKE THEE, SNOW, TO BE MY WEDDED WIFE, TO HAVE AND TO HOLD FROM THIS DAY FORWARD, FOR BETTER OR FOR WORSE, FOR RICHER OR POORER, IN SICKNESS AND IN HEALTH, TO LOVE AND TO CHERISH, TILL DEATH DO US PART, AND THEREUNTO I PLIGHT THEE MY TROTH.
FORASMUCH AS BIGBY AND SNOW HAVE CONSENTED TOGETHER IN HOLY WEDLOCK AND HAVE WITNESSED THE SAME BEFORE GOD AND THIS COMPANY, I PRONOUNCE THEREFORE THAT THEY BE MAN AND WIFE TOGETHER.

I TAKE THEE BIGBY, TO BE MY WEDDED ***HUSBAND,*** TO HAVE AND HOLD FROM THIS DAY FORWARD, FOR BETTER ORSE, FOR RICHER OR POORER, IN SICKNESS D IN HEALTH, TO LOVE AND TO CHERISH, TILL DEATH DO US PART, AND THEREUNTO I PLIGHT THEE MY TROTH.

YOU MAY KISS THE BRIDE.

SO THEY FEASTED.

AND TOASTED EACH OTHER.
TO THE FINEST MAN AND THE FINEST WOMAN IT HAS BEEN MY GOOD FORTUNE TO KNOW.

AND CELEBRATED THE JOYOUS DAY.
THAT'S ODD. HE DOES SEEM FAMILIAR--AS IF WE'D MET BEFORE.
WHERE ARE MOMMY AND DADDY GOING NOW?
SOME-WHERE YOU'RE NOT INVITED, WOLFLING.

EPILOGUE: MR. AND MRS. WOLF

Happily Ever After

BIG and small

In which we learn that Cinderella doesn't have three days, and a small infirmity has big consequences for our beloved Fabletown.

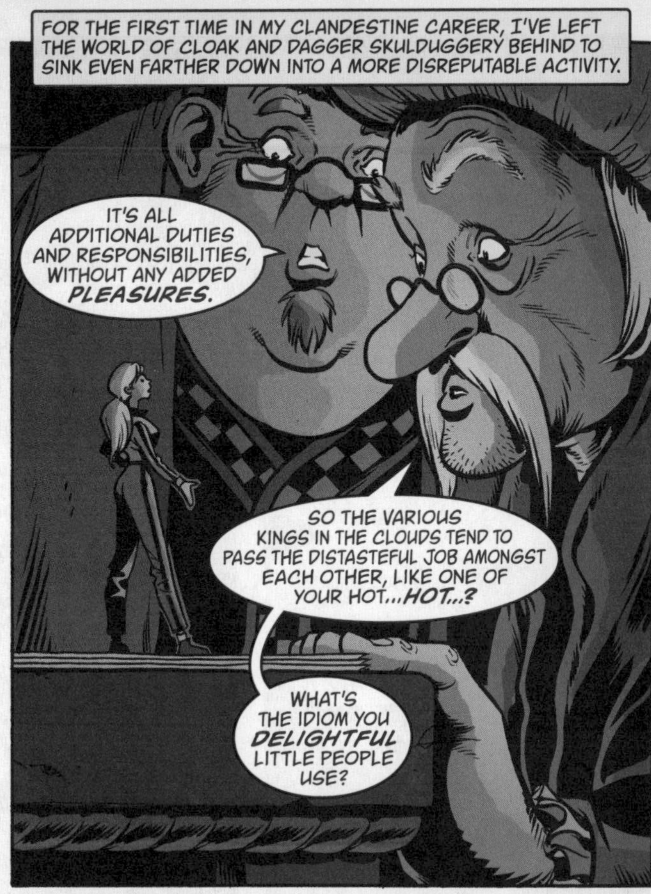

POLITICS.

A HOT POTATO.

AH, YES. SUCH A *COLORFUL* LANGUAGE.

IN ANY CASE, RUMBOLD IS HIGH KING FOR NOW, BUT HE CAN'T BE EXPECTED TO WORK WHEN HE DOESN'T FEEL WELL.

LORDY, HOW I *DO* HATE POLITICS.

BUT EVERYTHING'S BEEN NEGOTIATED, AND THIS TREATY BETWEEN FABLETOWN AND THE CLOUD KINGDOMS IS READY TO *SIGN!*

ONE QUICK DIP OF HIS ROYAL PEN AND OUR MONTHS OF WORK IS *COMPLETED!*

I'M NOT *NORMALLY* ONE TO SING MY OWN PRAISES, BUT IN THIS CASE IT'S TRUE. TREATING THIS DISEASE HAPPENS TO BE AMONG MY SPECIALTIES.

I HAVE TO MAKE THE PRESCRIBED SACRIFICES, PERFORM THE PROPER RITUAL PANTOMIME, AND CHANT THE SIX INDICATED PRAYERS.

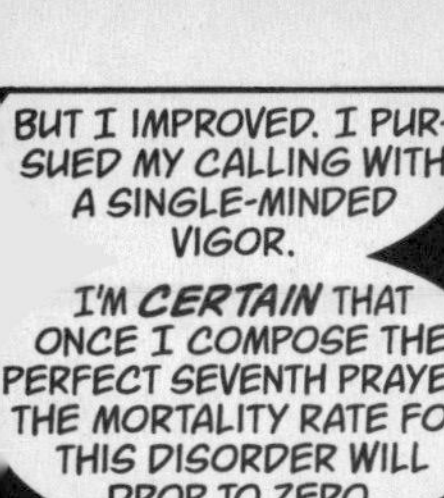

THE CLOUD KINGDOMS ARE DEFINITELY THE SAME PLACE AS *CLOUD CUCKOO LAND.*

ONLY FOR A FEW SECONDS.

I UNDERSTAND.

I'M NO DOCTOR, BUT THEN NEITHER IS *THIS* QUACK.

WHAT I AM IS A MODERN GIRL LIVING IN A MODERN WORLD. I'VE ABSORBED SOME BASIC SCIENCE THROUGH SIMPLE CULTURAL OSMOSIS.
I NEED A CLOSER LOOK.

ENOUGH TO KNOW A CURE FOR A SIMPLE EARACHE THAT TAKES A MONTH OR MORE IS NO CURE AT ALL.
EWWWW!
I SMELL PUS.

THIS IS OUTRAGEOUS!
I MUST INSIST THAT YOU LEAVE!
WHAT'S ALL THIS SCREAMING WHILE I'M TRYING TO SLEEP?
YIKES!

IT'S JUST ME, YOUR HIGHNESS-- YOUR HUMBLE LITTLE AMBASSADOR FROM FABLETOWN.

NOW LISTEN HERE, KING RUMBOLD. I APOLOGIZE FOR MY UNCOURTLY CANDOR, BUT I SUSPECT I WON'T HAVE TIME FOR THE USUAL DIPLOMATIC NICETIES.
I KNOW A REAL DOCTOR WHO CAN CURE WHAT AILS YOU. IN RETURN, YOU HAVE TO PROMISE ME THAT YOU WON'T HAND OVER YOUR KING-SHIP WHILE I GO FETCH HIM.
BUT--

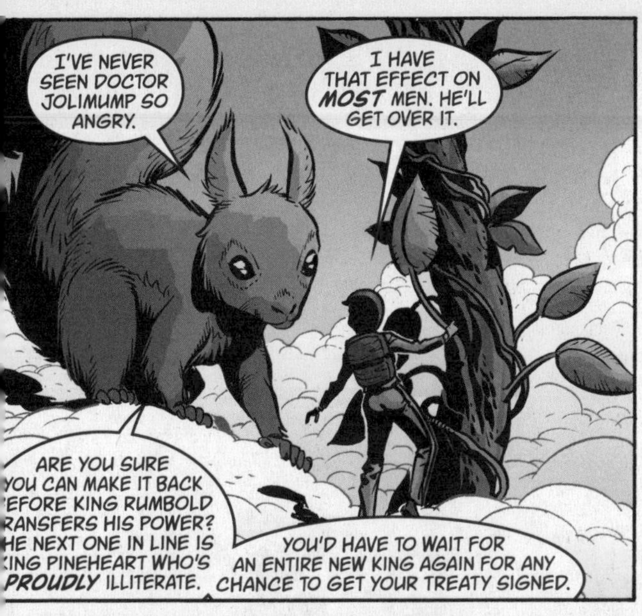

FIRST THING I DO, ONCE THIS NONSENSE IS ALL DONE, IS TRAP OUR HANDSOME SHERIFF IN HIS OFFICE AND LAY DOWN THE LAW.

NO MORE DIPLOMATIC MISSIONS! NOTHING BUT CLOAK AND DAGGER FROM NOW ON!

I'M A LOVELY SPY AND A HALFWAY DECENT ASSASSIN. BUT I AM ABSOLUTELY ONE CRAPPY POLITICIAN.

STILL, EVEN THIS JOB HAS ITS OCCASIONAL PLEASURES.

GERONIMO, BABY.

I UNDERSTAND BIGBY DIDN'T ENJOY THIS PART OF HIS BEANSTALK MISSION. DON'T TELL ANYONE BUT THE BIGGEST, BADDEST DENIZEN OF FABLETOWN HAS A PROFOUND DISLIKE--MAYBE EVEN *FEAR*--OF ANYTHING THAT TAKES HIS FEET OFF SOLID GROUND.
SILLY WOLF. THIS IS ABOUT AS *GLORIOUS* AS LIFE GETS.

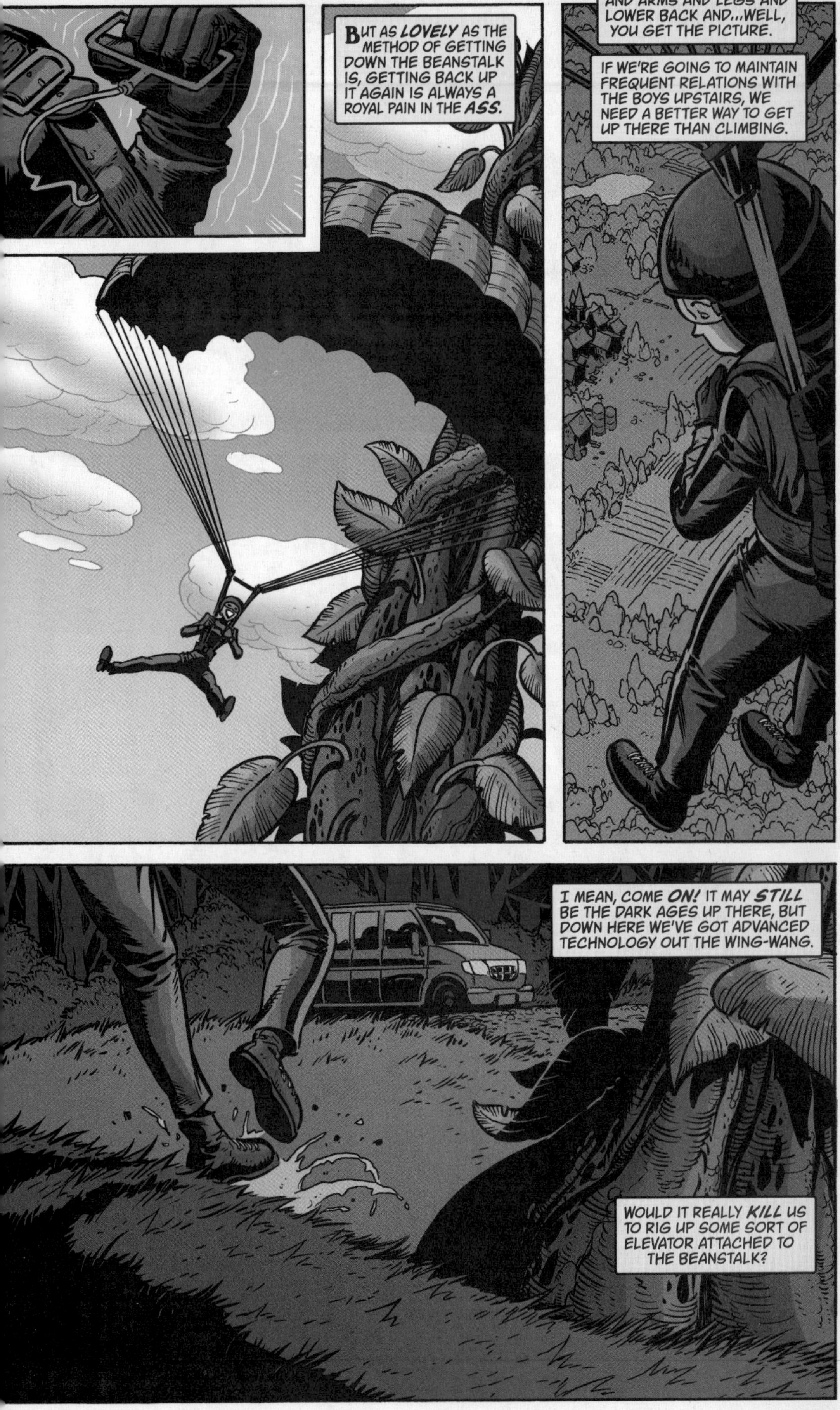

BUT AS *LOVELY* AS THE METHOD OF GETTING DOWN THE BEANSTALK IS, GETTING BACK UP IT AGAIN IS ALWAYS A ROYAL PAIN IN THE *ASS.*

I MEAN, COME *ON!* IT MAY *STILL* BE THE DARK AGES UP THERE, BUT DOWN HERE WE'VE GOT ADVANCED TECHNOLOGY OUT THE WING-WANG.

WOULD IT REALLY *KILL* US TO RIG UP SOME SORT OF ELEVATOR ATTACHED TO THE BEANSTALK?

YES, MIGHTY PRINCE OF MAYORS, THIS IS SOMETHING OF AN EMERGENCY. I'M ON MY WAY TO FABLETOWN. THEN I'LL NEED TO GET BACK TO THE FARM AS SOON AS POSSIBLE.

WHILE I'M EN ROUTE I NEED YOU TO FIND THE GOOD DOCTOR SWINEHEART AND HAVE HIM WAITING FOR ME. THEN I NEED YOU TO GET FRAU TOTENKINDER TO--
NO, FORMER LOVE OF MY LIFE, I AM NOT SIMPLY TRYING TO THROW MY WEIGHT AROUND.

OKAY, THAT'S NOT ENTIRELY TRUE. I AM THROWING MY WEIGHT AROUND A BIT. I HAVE TO CONFESS I LIKE MAKING MY EX-HUSBAND JUMP THROUGH HOOPS.
IT'S ANOTHER ONE OF THE RARE JOYS OF THIS JOB.
BECAUSE TIME IS WELL AND TRULY OF THE ESSENCE, THAT'S WHY.
HOURS LATER...
OF COURSE I CAN'T BE CERTAIN WITHOUT EXAMINING THE PATIENT DIRECTLY, BUT WHAT YOU'VE DESCRIBED SOUNDS LIKE A SIMPLE CASE OF OTITIS MEDIA WITH EFFUSION.

FABLETOWN.
CAN YOU GIVE THAT TO ME AGAIN IN ENGLISH?

HE HAS A COMMON EAR INFECTION WITH SOME FLUID BUILD-UP. GIVE HIM A FEW WEEKS TO A MONTH OF REST AND IT WILL CLEAR UP ON ITS OWN.
WE DON'T HAVE THAT KIND OF TIME, DOCTOR. THE CURRENT HIGH KING IS A BIG BABY WHO CAN'T TAKE ANY PAIN.
UNTIL HE FEELS BETTER, HE WON'T EVEN GET OUT OF BED LONG ENOUGH TO SIGN ONE DOCUMENT.

WE NEED A QUICK CURE.
WELL, I CAN GIVE YOU SOME ANTIBIOTIC EARDROPS AND A TUBE TO DRAIN THE FLUID, WHICH WILL SPEED UP HEALING TO A MATTER OF DAYS.
BUT THE TUBE HAS TO BE CAREFULLY PLACED OR IT WILL CAUSE MORE HARM THAN IT CURES. I'LL NEED ABOUT THREE DAYS TO TRAIN YOU HOW TO DO IT.

NO TIME. JUST POINT OUT THE RIGHT SPOT ON AN ANATOMICAL DIAGRAM. I HAVE AN IDEA TO MAKE SURE THE THING GETS PLACED IN EXACTLY THE RIGHT SPOT.
I'M SURE WE HAVE AN ANATOMY BOOK SOMEWHERE IN ALL OF THESE STACKS, RIGHT?

AND EVEN LATER...
IT TOOK SOME TIME TO ROUND UP MY NEXT APPOINTMENT, SO I SNUCK IN A SHOWER AND CHANGE OF CLOTHES.
THANK YOU FOR AGREEING TO SEE ME ON SUCH SHORT NOTICE, FRAU TOTENKINDER.

NOT AT ALL, CINDERELLA. IT'S MY PRIVILEGE TO SERVE FABLETOWN IN WHATEVER SMALL WAYS I CAN. BUT I'M NOT SURE WHY YOU NEED SOMETHING TO MAKE YOU SMALLER...
BECAUSE I'M STILL JUST A LITTLE TOO BIG TO FIT INSIDE A GIANT'S EAR.

WHAT AN ODD THING TO SAY.
BUT IT'S ACADEMIC BECAUSE I DON'T HAVE ANYTHING PREPARED THAT CAN SHRINK YOU. CONSTRUCTING A NEW SPELL IS *POSSIBLE,* BUT WOULD TAKE AT LEAST THREE DAYS TO--

I APOLOGIZE FOR INTERRUPTING BUT WE DON'T REALLY HAVE *DAYS.* THAT'S OKAY, THOUGH. THIS WAS A LONG SHOT ANYWAY.
OH, WE'RE NOT DONE YET, DEAR GIRL. THERE ARE *ALWAYS* OTHER OPTIONS TO EXPLORE. PERHAPS I DO HAVE SOMETHING THAT MIGHT SUBSTITUTE.

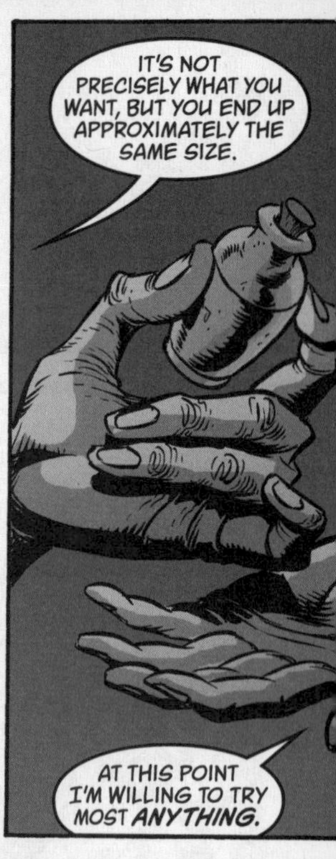
IT'S NOT PRECISELY WHAT YOU WANT, BUT YOU END UP APPROXIMATELY THE SAME SIZE.
AT THIS POINT I'M WILLING TO TRY MOST *ANYTHING.*

WITHIN AN HOUR I'M ON THE ROAD AGAIN ON MY WAY BACK UP TO THE FARM.
ROSE RED, THIS IS CINDY. WHAT ARE THE RULES FOR SOME-ONE MY SIZE VISITING SMALLTOWN?
I HAVE A BACKUP PLAN. I *ALWAYS* HAVE A BACKUP PLAN, BECAUSE I'M JUST THAT GOOD.

THREE DAYS' TRAINING? I'M NOT GOING TO *STOMP* ON ANYONE. AND WHY DOES EVERYTHING IN THIS CAPER TAKE *THREE DAYS?*

THREE DAYS TO LEARN HOW TO PLACE A DRAINAGE TUBE! THREE DAYS TO BUILD A SHRINKING SPELL! THREE DAYS TO LEARN HOW **NOT** TO STEP ON TINY PEOPLE!
GODS ABOVE, WILL EVERYONE **PLEASE** GET IT THROUGH YOUR COLLECTIVE SKULL THAT **I... DON'T...HAVE... THREE... DAYS!**

ALBANY
THIS EXIT
NO, ROSE, I'M SORRY. I WASN'T SPECIFICALLY YELLING AT **YOU.** IT'S THE ENTIRE **UNIVERSE** THAT'S PISSING ME OFF RIGHT NOW.

A FEW HOURS LATER...
TRUST ME. I WON'T BE **BIG** ENOUGH TO STOMP ON ANYONE.

JUST GUIDE ME TO THE EDGE OF THEIR TERRITORY AND I'LL TAKE IT FROM THERE, ROSE.
AND I'M WILLING TO TAKE YOUR WORD ON THIS **WHY** EXACTLY?

BECAUSE I'M SMART AND LOVELY AND CLEARLY THE LEADING LADY OF THIS PARTICULAR TALE. AND MY HEART, AS ALWAYS, IS **PURE.**
AND BECAUSE OUR SECRET TREATY WITH THE CLOUD KINGDOMS IS ON THE LINE.

YES. I'LL SEND FOR HIM.

NOT *YET.* I NEED YOU TO STAY RIGHT HERE AND WAIT FOR MY RETURN. ONCE I DRINK THIS I WON'T BE ABLE TO GET AROUND TOO WELL IN THE NORMAL-SIZED WORLD.

NO GULLIVERS BEYOND THIS POINT

WOW.
WOW INDEED.
CINDY?
I ASSUMED THE TRANSFORMATION WOULD BE MORE GRADUAL.
IN ALL OF MY PAST MISSIONS, NO MATTER HOW STRANGE THEY GOT--AND BELIEVE ME, SOME WERE WELL AND TRULY WEIRD--AT LEAST I REMAINED HUMAN THROUGHOUT.
THIS IS SO BIZARRE!
EVERYTHING IS SO BIG!
THIS IS A TOTALLY NEW EXPERIENCE FOR ME, AND IT'S NOT BAD.
I WONDER IF THEY HAVE ANYTHING THAT CAN TRANSFORM ME INTO A BIRD?
I'LL BE RIGHT BACK!

BEING ABLE TO FLY UNDER MY OWN POWER WOULD BE UNDENIABLY HELPFUL ON SOME OF MY MISSIONS--
--NOT TO MENTION HOW UNBELIEVABLY COOL IT WOULD BE.

HALT!
YIKES!

WHO GOES THERE?
UHM--HI, I WAS JUST--YOU KNOW-- HEADING INTO SMALLTOWN TO UHM--
WELL, CORPORAL CLIVE, SHE CAN TALK, SO SHE'S OBVIOUSLY A FABLE MOUSE. BUT I'VE NEVER SEEN HER BEFORE.

SO, YOU'RE NOT A RESIDENT OF SMALLTOWN? AND YOU AREN'T A MEMBER OF THE MOUNTED POLICE?
NO, I'M-- WELL, THIS IS GOING TO SOUND A BIT ODD, BUT--
MOVE ALONG, STRANGER.

NO, OFFICER, I WON'T BE MOVING ALONG.
WHAT I AM GOING TO DO IS PROCEED WITH YOUR GUIDANCE INTO SMALL-TOWN, WHERE YOU'RE GOING TO POINT OUT YOUR TOWN MEDIC TO ME.
YOU CAN'T ORDER US AROUND!

YES, IN FACT I CAN. I HAVE ALL SORTS OF AUTHORITY TO PUSH YOU BOTH AROUND, OR FOLD, SPINDLE OR MUTILATE YOU TO MY HEART'S CONTENT.
BUT I DON'T WANT TO DO THAT. NOR DO I WANT TO LET YOU IN ON ANY OF THE DETAILS OF MY MISSION FOR YOUR OWN GOOD.

SEE? IF I WERE TO SPILL MY SECRETS AND TELL YOU ENOUGH TO CONVINCE YOU OF MY AUTHORITY, YOU'D SUDDENLY HAVE WHAT'S KNOWN AS HIGH SECURITY CLEARANCE.
AND THAT WOULD CHANGE YOUR LIVES IN WAYS THAT--TRUST ME--YOU WOULDN'T WANT.

AT THE VERY LEAST YOU'D HAVE TO QUIT THE MOUSE POLICE AND LEAVE SMALLTOWN--PROBABLY FOREVER. YOU'D CERTAINLY NEVER GET TO TALK TO ANY OF YOUR FRIENDS AND FAMILY AGAIN.

YOU'D PROBABLY IVE OUT THE REST F YOUR LIVES IN A ERY SMALL BOX SOMEWHERE IN THE WOODLAND BUSINESS OFFICE.
SO, SINCE YOU WOULDN'T WANT THAT TO HAPPEN TO YOU AND I WOULDN'T WANT TO DO THAT TO YOU, HERE'S WHAT WE'RE GOING TO DO INSTEAD.

YOU'RE GOING TO ESCORT ME--UNDER GUARD IF YOU INSIST--INTO TOWN TO MEET YOUR LOCAL MEDIC.
THEN, WHEN I'M DONE TALKING TO HIM, YOU'LL ESCORT BOTH OF US BACK THIS WAY.
HAVE I MADE MYSELF CLEAR, GENTLEMEN?

THE MOUNTED POLICE COP EVENTUALLY LISTENED TO REASON--WHICH IS GOOD, BECAUSE MY BACKUP PLAN IN THIS CASE WAS TO DISABLE THE TWO OF THEM AND GO ON MY WAY.
THE TROUBLE IS I'VE NEVER HAD TO FIGHT AS A LITTLE BROWN *MOUSE* BEFORE. I'VE BEEN TRAINED IN ALL SORTS OF WAYS TO INFLICT VIOLENCE.
BUT THOUGH I HAD NO DOUBT I COULD GET THE BETTER OF THEM, I WASN'T POSITIVE I HAD LEARNED ENOUGH CONTROL OVER MY PRESENT FORM TO DO IT WITHOUT KILLING THEM.
I DON'T HAVE A LOT OF TIME TO EXPLAIN, DOC, BUT HERE'RE THE BASIC DETAILS.
I'M NOT REALLY A MOUSE. I'M A GULLIVER-SIZED FABLE UNDER A SPELL THAT WILL WEAR OFF IN A DAY OR TWO. BEFORE THAT HAPPENS, YOU AND I HAVE A *LOT* OF WORK TO DO.
I NEED YOU TO ACCOMPANY ME ON A BIG ADVENTURE WHERE I'M GOING TO HEL YOU TREAT A VERY BIG PATIENT WHO HAS A VERY BIG EARACHE.

I'VE GOT THE MEDICINE AND TOOLS WE NEED, AND OUR TRANSPORTATION IS BEING ARRANGED.
I'M SORRY I HAVE TO RECRUIT YOU, DOC. I WAS ORIGINALLY PLANNING TO DO THIS JOB MYSELF.
DR. ROBERT SMALLISH
OFFICE HOURS 10 to 2 Monday-Friday
BUT, AS YOU CAN SEE, I NO LONGER HAVE THE HANDS FOR WHAT MIGHT TURN OUT TO BE A DELICATE MEDICAL PROCEDURE.
THEREFORE, YOU'VE JUST VOLUNTEERED.
BUT--
THE WALL SURROUNDING OUR LANDS IS JUST BEYOND THIS UNDERBRUSH AHEAD, MA'AM.
THEN I'LL THANK YOU NOW, CORPORAL CLIVE, AND INVITE YOU TO BE ON YOUR WAY. YOU DON'T NEED TO SEE WHAT HAPPENS FROM NOW ON.
THERE YOU ARE! I WAS GETTING WORRIED.
I IMAGINE YOU'VE ALREADY MET ROSE RED, DOCTOR.
I HOPE YOU DON'T MIND FLYING, DOC. WE'RE TOO SMALL AND DON'T HAVE TIME FOR A LONG CLIMB.

LATER THAT SAME DAY...

DON'T BE SCARED, DOC. COMMANDER ARROW HAS CARRIED PASSENGERS MANY TIMES BEFORE AND NEVER DROPPED A *ONE* OF THEM, RIGHT, COMMANDER?

I HAVE A PERFECT SAFETY RECORD, MISS CINDERELLA.

WHAT DID YOU SAY? I CAN BARELY *HEAR* YOU!

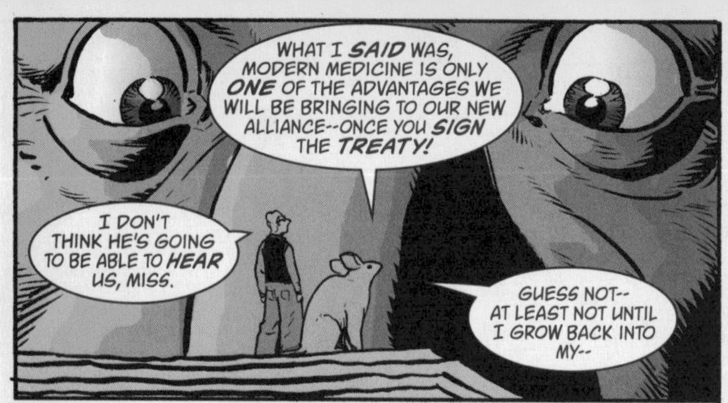
WHAT I SAID WAS, MODERN MEDICINE IS ONLY ONE OF THE ADVANTAGES WE WILL BE BRINGING TO OUR NEW ALLIANCE--ONCE YOU SIGN THE TREATY!
I DON'T THINK HE'S GOING TO BE ABLE TO HEAR US, MISS.
GUESS NOT-- AT LEAST NOT UNTIL I GROW BACK INTO MY--

URP!
I THINK I MAY BE ABOUT TO--

YOW!
OH MY GOODNESS! YOU'RE A GIANT!
ZOUNDS!

A TINY NAKED MIRACLE APPEARS BEFORE US!
UHM-- DO ANY OF YOU GENTLEMEN HAVE A HANKY I COULD BORROW?

OF COURSE I MADE TWO ENEMIES THAT DAY. GUSTROLF DIDN'T LIKE ME GOING BEHIND HIS BACK, AND DOCTOR JOLIMUMP DIDN'T LIKE BEING EXPOSED AS A FRAUD.

HAT I DIDN'T TELL THEM
ID WON'T INCLUDE IN MY
FICIAL REPORT) IS THE
CE FRAU TOTENKINDER
ARGED ME FOR HER
GIC POTION, WHEN SHE
EW SHE HAD ME OVER
A BARREL.

THAT'S CERTAINLY GOING TO COME BACK TO HAUNT ME.

THE END

SPECIAL TRAVEL SUPPLEMENT

Maps of the Fable Territories in the Mundane World
With Places of Interest and Historical Locations Noted

FABLETOWN

1 The Grand Green Florist. The Château D'if Fencing Academy is directly above.
2 Edward Bear's Candies. Try the honey clusters. They're famous.
3 Ford Laundry (and dry cleaning). The washer woman at the Ford may not be pleasant, but she gets all sorts of stains out.
4 Nod's Books. Including a comics nook.
5 Lewis' Antiques. Wondrous items at reasonable rates.
6 I Am The Eggman Diner. Try the apple pancakes and do feel free to call it the Eggman for short.
7 The Yellow Brick Roadhouse (also extending up to the second floor). Food and drink at reasonable rates.
8 The Webb 'n' Muffet Market. Delivery boy wanted.
9 The Woodland's front courtyard.
10 The Woodland's garden. A nice quiet spot to sit and ponder whodunit.
11 The Woodland Building. It's bigger inside than out.
12 The Glass Slipper Shoe Store. High prices, but quality goods.
13 The Branstock Tavern. Fabletown's favorite watering hole.

A) This is the alley where Jack was mugged by the three wooden soldiers.
B) Three blocks to The Empire's New Embassy on Andersen Street.
C) Five and a half blocks to Rodney and June Greenwood's apartment.

NORTH!
MERMAID PON
TO FABLETOW
the farm
LIVESTOCK FIELDS
FARMLAND
MAIN VILLAGE

Wolf Valley
WOLF MANOR
SHERE KHAN'S GRAVE
GRASSLANDS
THE SECRET BEANSTALK
SMALLTOWN
The Great Wood

Happily Ever After:

THE COMPLETE SCRIPT TO FABLES #50

Fables

Issue Fifty

Title: Happily Ever After

By Bill Willingham

48 Pages

Artist and Lettering Note: In a break from tradition, the main titles and credits for this issue will appear in the back of the book, rather than the front. However, there will be chapter titles and we'd like them all in the same general font as the main title.

Page One (five panels)

Panel One

This isn't really a panel. It's the space you need to leave at the top of the page for this section's chapter title.

Display Lettering: Chapter One: Secret Agent Man

Panel Two

It's early morning. We see a lonely two-lane (at most) dirt road somewhere in upstate New York. This is far away from any sign of civilization or habitation. Two sets of cars are parked in the middle of this road, facing each other from a distance of about thirty feet from each other — sort of like when competing underworld families have a clandestine meeting in an out-of-the-way place. One of the sets of cars consists of Prince Charming's sports car, in the lead, followed by another, less expensive sedan, followed by a paneled van, like the type of van a professional janitorial service might use — except this one has no distinguishing markings. The van is in the rear of this set of cars. About thirty feet away from them, facing them, is the other set of cars, which in fact is just a single undistinguished sedan. A small group of people are on foot, meeting each other, in the road, midway between each of the sets of cars. From this distance it won't be possible to tell who these people are, but they are: Bigby; Mowgli; Prince Charming; Beast; and Rose Red. One other note: An even rougher dirt road branches off from this road, at about where the cars are parked. This second road is hardly a road at all — more like two parallel wheel ruts carved out of the grass and weeds and brush. This road looks more like a medieval wooded cart road than one used by modern vehicles. It leads off the main dirt road and goes towards the deep forest area of the Farm. It's a cool, late summer morning.

Non Narration Cap: A lonely side road on the outskirts of the Farm — Fabletown's annex in upstate New York.

Voice (from group of people): Welcome home, Bigby. We've missed you.

2nd Voice (from same group): Farm's never been my home, Mr. Mayor. This is as close as I've been to it.

Panel Three

Now we move in closer to the small cluster of people. Bigby and Mowgli have walked up from the single car, to join Prince Charming, Beast and Rose Red, who've come up from the line of cars. They're all dressed for the cool morning and for tramping about in the rough. Bigby is dressed in the same black T-shirt, hiking shorts and hiking boots that he was wearing in the Storybook Love story arc. He's close enough to civilization that he's smoking again. Bigby looks unimpressed with this gathering.

Charming: Fair enough. In any case, thank you for agreeing to return.

Bigby: Considering Bagheera's freedom depended on it, I didn't really have much choice, did I?

Mowgli: I hope you realize how much Baggy and I appreciate it.

Panel Four

Another shot of the group, as Charming leads Bigby to the van at the end of the line of cars. The others follow.

Charming: I imagine you'll want to see Snow and your kids before —

Bigby: Nope. If this secret mission of yours goes bad, why cause them the extra grief and worry? Let's get it done first.

Charming: Then follow me to the van and we'll be on our way.

Panel Five

We return to a wide shot, overhead view, looking down at the parked cars, as the van pulls around the car in front of it and bumps its way over the edge of the road onto the rougher (wooden cart track) road, headed towards the woods. Basically everyone is in the one van now, leaving the other cars where they're parked.

Voice (from van): Pardon the bad road, but we're headed to the most remote and restricted section of the Farm.

Page Two (one panel)

Panel One

This is a full-page splash. In the foreground we see the tiny van heading along the bumpy, twisty forest road, towards something huge in the background. In the background we see a giant magic beanstalk rising from the forest and reaching clear off the top of the page, going all the way up into the sky. The base of the beanstalk is huge — as big around as the base of giant redwood trees. But unlike such trees the beanstalk is a twisted rope of several impossibly-thick strands imperfectly twined together. All kinds of thick stems reach out from the main stalk, some just ending in a curl of stem and some ending in huge leaves — big enough that a grown human can bunk in one like it was a hammock (which is important in a few pages). This beanstalk is in a very remote area of the Farm. No part of the civilized part of the Farm can be seen from here. In fact, no sign of civilization (except the van and the bad road) can be seen at all.

Voice (from van): Wow! That's a —

2nd Voice (from van): That's right, Rose Red, it's a beanstalk — one of the magic ones from Jack's original magic bean stash.

Same 2nd Voice (connected balloon): Which is why we never paid much attention to Jack when he claimed to still have some of the beans. He didn't know we had them all along.

Page Three (five panels)

Panel One

The van pulls up near the base of the beanstalk. The side door opens and we see Rose Red getting out, followed by Beast. Rose Red keeps looking up at the giant stalk, amazement and disbelief in her eyes.

Rose Red: So this is what you've been up to out here for the past two years? All the secret comings and goings? Why didn't you tell me?

Beast: Until now, you didn't need to know.

Panel Two

Now all of the crew: Charming, Bigby, Mowgli, Rose Red and Beast are out of the van and standing near the base of the beanstalk. Everyone else seems unimpressed, except Rose Red who can't stop looking up at it.

Beast: Bigby taught me that much. Compartmentalization is the be all and end all of the spook game. No one *gets* to know unless they absolutely *need* to know.

Bigby: Basic operational doctrine, kid.

Panel Three

Closer on Rose Red. She's starting to freak out.

Rose Red: But this - !

Rose Red: You can't - !

Rose Red: It sticks out like a sore thumb! A *giant* sore thumb! This is going to attract all kinds of mundy attention to the Farm!

Panel Four

Beast lays some calming (not intimate) hands on Rose Red.

Beast: Not at all. It's completely imaginary until you get close enough.

Beast: No one can see it from a distance. A mundy pilot can fly within 300 feet of it and never know it's there.

Panel Five

Wider shot. Rose is calmer now, but still impressed by the sight of the beanstalk. Bigby looks up at it too, but for a different reason. He's judging the spaces between leaf stems (which are as thick as a normal tree's branches), to see if he can climb it without ropes and climbing gear. They are indeed close enough to free climb, by the way.

Charming: And since no flight paths pass within twenty miles of this place, we're fine.

Beast: The beanstalk's basic structure is transdimensional.

Page Four (five panels)

Panel One

Another group shot, concentrating on Charming, who's still teaching Rose Red about beanstalk lore, and Bigby, who looks at Charming.

Charming: Though the roots are firmly in our world, somewhere along the way it ends up poking its way into the Cloud Kingdoms.

Bigby: This is all very informative, but can we get to the practical business?

Panel Two

Bigby looks back up at the beanstalk, flicking his cigarette away as he does so. The closest leaf stems (branches) are well over his head. Beast at least is in this shot as well.

Bigby: I assume I'm going to climb this thing?

Beast: Exactly.

Bigby: Where's my gear?

Panel Three

Same basic shot, but including Charming now as well.

Charming: It's waiting for you upstairs, along with your specific instructions. We thought it better that way, to further guard against anything leaking out.

Beast: Your contact will meet you at the top.

Panel Four

Bigby leaps up and grabs the lowest leaf stem, hanging from it. Rose Red can be seen in the group below him.

Bigby: Then I might as well get started.

Rose Red: Are you sure there isn't anything you want me to tell Snow?

Bigby: I'm sure, Rose.

Panel Five

Now Bigby easily pulls himself up on the leaf stem he was hanging from. He's begun his climb. It's still pretty early in the morning.

Bigby: If I don't return, I was never here in the first place.

Bigby: If I do, I can tell her myself.

Page Five (four panels)

Panel One

We switch scenes slightly to follow Bigby on his climb up into the sky. In this panel he's pretty damned high, but we can still see the forested land far below him. Maybe now we can see some of the familiar details of the Farm off in the distance. Bigby is climbing pretty steadily, keeping a good pace, without getting tired. It's still daytime.

No captions or dialogue in this panel.

Panel Two

Same scene, but hours later. Now there is nothing but cloud below Bigby. He's passed through at least one cloud layer and is still going strong. The beanstalk is still as big around as a giant redwood tree trunk.

No captions or dialogue in this panel.

Panel Three

It's nighttime and Bigby is sleeping comfortably in one of the giant beanstalk leaves (see, I told you it would be important), which easily holds his weight. It's big enough that he could roll over a couple of times and still have no worry about falling.

No captions or dialogue in this panel.

Panel Four

It's another day and Bigby is climbing again. It's so high up now that snow is falling. Since Bigby doesn't feel the cold he just keeps climbing away.

No captions or dialogue in this panel.

Page Six (five panels)

Panel One

We switch scene to another daytime establishing shot of the Farm — this time we see that part of the Farm we normally see, with the central village area. It's daytime.

Voice (from town square): Wake up, Bagheera, it's emancipation day for all imprisoned Fables of the black pantheresque persuasion.

Panel Two

We move down into the Farm's town square, and the big tiger cage that's been the centerpiece of the town for far too many issues. Prince Charming, Mowgli, Rose Red and Boy Blue are all there, as Rose has just unlocked the cage and is swinging the cage door wide open. Charming is holding up some sort of official-looking document in his hands. Mowgli and Boy Blue simply look happy. Charming, Mowgli and Rose Red are dressed differently than they were at the beginning of this issue, to show that this is not the same day. Bagheera is in his cage, yawning with sleep and only tentatively moving towards the open doorway, as if he doesn't quite believe he's free.

Bagheera: Really? I'm free to go?

Mowgli: You're officially sprung, buddy.

Charming: Here's your pardon — signed and sealed.

Panel Three

Bagheera springs out of the cage right onto Mowgli's chest, flattening him onto his back, onto the ground. Even though the wind's knocked out of him, Mowgli is still grinning like a fool. Bagheera is obviously quite happy and this is no attack — it's roughhousing with a good friend.

Bagheera: I can go anywhere I want?

Charming: Anywhere on the Farm, at least.

Mowgli: Get off of me, you giant rat!

Panel Four

Now, like a bullet, Bagheera springs into action, running for the edge of town, heading full speed towards the nearest forest areas. The others watch him as he goes. Blue is helping Mowgli get up off of the ground. Charming is shouting at Bagheera's retreating back.

Charming: Anywhere not restricted, that is!

Blue: Where's he off to like a rocket?

Rose Red: Someplace that doesn't resemble a cage, I imagine.

Panel Five

Bagheera is long gone, leaving only a cloud of dust in his wake. Rose Red looks at the cage, while Blue talks to Mowgli as he dusts himself off.

Rose Red: Speaking of which, let's get this thing dismantled today. It's been a blight on our town square for entirely too long.

Blue: He'll probably remember to thank you, once he's settled down a bit.

Mowgli: I expect.

Page Seven (four panels)

Panel One

This isn't really a panel. It's the space you need to leave at the top of the page for this section's chapter title.

Display Lettering: Chapter Two: Castles in the Sky

Panel Two

We switch scenes back to Bigby, who's just reached the top of his climb. This is from the point of view of the Cloud Kingdoms, which is basically a land in the sky whose land is all the top side of fluffy white clouds. In this panel we see a fairly close shot of the very top strands of the beanstalk — which have gotten pretty small in diameter by now — twining and twisting, poking through the top of the billowing clouds, ending just about twelve feet above the clouds. We can just see one of Bigby's arms reaching out of the clouds for his next handhold of beanstalk. It is daytime but we can't see too many details of the land yet.

Non Narration Cap: Three days later...

Bigby (from cloud): I better be near the top. I'm running out of beanstalk.

Panel Three

We pull back just a bit farther to see that Bigby has now climbed to the very top of the beanstalk, which is thin enough that it can barely hold his weight now. Bigby is about four or five feet off the "ground" of the billowing cloudscape around him. He's clutching the beanstalk pretty tight, not willing to jump down and test his weight on the cloud tops. A voice talks from behind Bigby (off panel), but Bigby can't turn to see who it is without shifting his weight on his precarious perch. For the first time ever we might even see a small bit of fright on Bigby's face (not too much fright — more like just some advanced nervousness).

Voice (from off-panel behind Bigby): Yes, you're at the top, Bigby.

Bigby: Who's that? I don't think I can turn around without shifting too much weight. This thing's ready to snap off under me as it is.

Panel Four

This is the big panel of the page. We now pull out to see a wide shot of Bigby and the surrounding area. Cinderella (Cindy) is standing on the rolling cloud tops, right behind Bigby. She's dressed for outdoor living — perhaps in some variation of the track-suit thingie she was wearing when we last saw her (in the Mean Seasons story arc, when she was helping Bigby and Beast interrogate the wooden heads). Behind Cindy we can see that she has a small tent and semi-permanent campsite set up, all pitched on one of the hills of the rolling cloudscape. She's clearly been camping out here for awhile, near the top of the beanstalk, waiting for someone to arrive from below. In the background all we can see so far is a rolling landscape of cloud tops, with a clear blue sky above it. Cindy looks a bit amused to see Bigby looking so nervous.

Cindy: You can step down now, Bigby. The cloudscape is solid beneath you.

Bigby: It wasn't when I was climbing up through it.

Bigby: Is that you, Cindy?

Page Eight (five panels)

Panel One

Closer on Cindy, as she smiles up at Bigby, still clinging to the beanstalk. She's having fun teasing him. Maybe we can also see Bigby's feet in this panel — at about head height to Cindy — wrapped securely around the stalk.

Cindy: Yes, it's me, and you really can get down. It's solid from the top, even though you could pass through from below. That's the way the enchantment works.

Cindy: Honestly, I don't think I've ever seen you afraid of anything before, Bigby.

Panel Two

Closer on Bigby, still clinging to his perch. He looks a bit cranky now at what Cindy said in teasing him.

Bigby: And you still haven't. Nervous isn't the same as scared.

Bigby: Remember, me and mine didn't evolve from monkeys like you and yours. I don't have climbing hardwired into me from a million generations past.

Panel Three

Wider shot as Cindy bounces up and down on the bit of cloud nearest to where the beanstalk has thrust through — to show Bigby it's safe and he won't fall through. She's still smiling, enjoying this moment.

Cindy: Point taken, but you really can get down. See? I'm jumping up and down right next to you without falling through.

Cindy: Trust me. I've been living up here for months, preparing the way for you with the locals.

Panel Four

Bigby is finally risking a look down to the cloud tops just below him. He's screwing up his courage to jump down from the beanstalk.

Cindy: There's really no need to be scared.

Bigby: Nervous.

Cindy: Right. Nervous. That's what I said.

Panel Five

Bigby finally lets go and falls the few short feet to the cloud top landscape below him. Cindy deftly steps out of the way. She's still smiling and still teasing him.

Bigby: Okay, here goes nothing.

Cindy: If you *do* fall through, you'll have a long time to regret listening to me on the way down.

Page Nine (five panels)

Panel One

Now Bigby stands up on wobbly feet. He looks like he's trying to stand on a very soft, constantly-shifting surface. Cindy, having gotten used to the footing long ago, stands just fine.

Bigby: Very funny. You've got quite the cruel streak in you, Cindy.

Cindy: Which is why we always got along so well. How does it feel?

Bigby: Shifty. Like trying to stand on a ground made of damp sponge.

Panel Two

Cindy watches as Bigby tries to stand, like a drunk man, nearly falling over with every minor shift of his weight.

Cindy: Yeah, it's odd, but you'll get used to it. It didn't take me much more than a day up here to get my sea legs — or cloud legs, actually.

Cindy: Truth is, since this is a giant land with giant distances, you won't be doing much walking up here anyway.

Panel Three

Cindy turns and calls out, and a giant squirrel's head suddenly appears, popping up from behind the next hump of cloud. This squirrel is big enough for both Bigby and Cindy to ride if they needed to (but they won't). This is a land of the giants and this squirrel, named Radiskop, is to scale with everything and everyone they are about to encounter. Bigby is a little taken aback by the sudden appearance of the huge beast.

Cindy: Radiskop!

Radiskop: Yes, Cinderella?

Cindy: Can you go inform our host the guest of honor has arrived?

Radiskop: You betcha!

Panel Four

Radiskop the giant squirrel goes bounding away from (us) Cindy and Bigby, enthusiastically leaping and bouncing off the sponge-like cloud as if it were a series of puffy trampolines.

Bigby: He seems enthusiastic.

Cindy: Rady's a big sweetheart.

Bigby: Big is right — big enough to swallow us both in two or three bites.

Panel Five

Wider shot. Radiskop is gone. Cindy turns back towards her campsite. Bigby follows behind her on very shaky legs.

Cindy: Help me break camp, while we wait for our transport to arrive.

Cindy: We won't be coming back this way.

Page Ten (four panels)

Panel One

This is the big panel of the page, taking up at least half of the page. We switch scenes to a shot of a giant named Humberjon striding across this vast, cloudy land. Humberjon is a young giant — basically a teenage boy. He's only going to be seen on this page, and one other panel later, so you can design him pretty much any way you like. As he walks, Humberjon is holding one arm out, with his palm up. Cinderella and Bigby are riding in that open palm, high above the cloudy ground below. All of Cindy's camping gear is packed up, rolled up and riding in the giant's open palm along with them. Note that there needs to be lots of gear shown — because it includes all of Cindy's camping gear plus all of the gear Bigby will be taking with him into the Homelands on his mission (the specifics of which are described in a few pages). Basically we need to see lots of stuff here. Humberjon is walking towards a big, dark wizard's castle (a giant wizard's castle) in the background. Also, now that we have a high vantage point, we can see other castles and towns scattered in the distance. It's still daytime.

Non Narration Cap: Less than an hour later…

Cindy (from giant's hand): Young Humberjon is taking us to the wizard Ulmore's castle. That's our staging area for the mission.

Bigby (from giant's hand): Nice view.

Panel Two

Closer on Cindy and Bigby riding in the giant's open palm. Cindy hands Bigby a multi-page document bound together with little brass fasteners (which we call brads over here on our side of the pond) - bound like movie screenplays are bound. This is the written mission plan that Bigby has to read and memorize. It's at least twenty pages thick.

Cindy: Here. We'll be awhile getting there, so you can start reading. These are your mission orders.

Panel Three

Same scene. Bigby starts reading.

Cindy: You'll have to memorize all of your instructions before you go. We can't let you take the physical documents with you.

Bigby: Standard procedure.

Panel Four

Closer on Bigby who is deep into reading the document now.

Lettering Note: Todd: From now on (until about halfway through this issue) all captions, unless otherwise noted, are the written instructions that Bigby is reading or has memorized for his mission. Can we have a serif font for these captions, please? Not a fake typewriter font though, since Fabletown is modern enough not to use old-fashioned typewriters anymore. Thanks.

Cap (mission text): Operation: *Israel*. Stage One: Preparation.

Cap (mission text): You will make contact with your Mission Operator at the summit, who will direct you to friendly elements in the Cloud Kingdoms.

Page Eleven (four panels)

Panel One

We switch scenes to an exterior shot of the wizard's giant castle. Some time has passed and so it's nighttime now. We can see a light showing from one of the higher tower windows.

Cap (mission text): Your primary contact among the giants will be the wizard Ulmore, who will prepare you for insertion.

Voice (from lighted tower window): Since you're not a magician, I'll have to try to explain things to you in layman's terms.

Panel Two

Big panel. Now we switch scenes inside the giant tower room to see the wizard Ulmore seated at a wooden table with a candlestick set on it, with a lit candle burning in it. The tiny forms of Cinderella and Bigby are seated on the table, looking up at Ulmore's giant face. Ulmore has to lean down to hear them, just the way Prince Charming had to lean close to hear his Mouse Police spies in the Storybook Love arc. Basically the giants are on the same scale to Bigby and Cindy as normal-sized Fables are to Lilliputian-sized Fables.

Cap (mission text): Extreme care should be taken not to do or say anything that might jeopardize the new and fragile diplomatic relations between Fabletown and the Cloud Kingdoms.

Ulmore: Even though the Cloud Kingdoms exist in their own dimension, in a seemingly paradoxical way they also exist in the sky over every known world.

Panel Three

Closer on Ulmore and the two Fables on the table.

Cap (mission text): Securing them as allies is vastly more important than the needs of this particular mission.

Ulmore: There's a corresponding location up here for any location down below, whether in your Mundy world or any world of the Empire.

Ulmore: Our task, then, is to find the location that looks down on their imperial capital.

Panel Four

Same scene.

Bigby: And just drop down on them from above?

Ulmore: Precisely. So far, the only way to bridge dimensions from below, coming upwards, is to travel via one of the magic beanstalks.

Page Twelve (four panels)

Panel One

Same scene. The candlelight conversation between Ulmore, Bigby and Cinderella continues.

Ulmore: That's kept us safe so far from the Adversary's armies.

Ulmore: But the dimensional doorways are always open going in the other direction.

Panel Two

We switch scenes to another part of the cloud kingdom. The giant wizard Ulmore is kneeling next to a large hole in the cloud floor being dug by the giant boy Humberjon, wielding a giant spade. Bigby and Cinderella are standing in one of Ulmore's open palms. Bigby is now laden down with all sorts of equipment. He is wearing a huge backpack of gear high on his back. Just below that (at about small-of-the-back or butt height) is strapped the first of two parachute packs. This is his main chute pack. On his belly is strapped his reserve parachute pack. Held in his arms is a fourth big bag of gear, called a musette bag. Once he makes his parachute jump, Bigby will release the musette bag, which will drop below him to be suspended about ten feet below him by two long straps, so that this bag will hit the ground before Bigby does and that loss of weight will allow Bigby's chute to slow down a tad bit more in the important few feet before landfall.

Here's some photo reference for a modern musette bag, but this is a small one. The one Bigby is carrying needs to be about twice as big and with longer straps: http://www.gr8gear.com/index.asp?PageAction=VIEWPROD&ProdID=3469

Here's a shot from the TV series Band of Brothers that shows some of the parachute troops beginning to strap on all of the gear they'll be taking with them for their D-Day jump. Note the very large musette bag on the ground in front of one of the troops: http://www.wingsamerica.com/webart/products/small/579.jpg

Here's a close-up shot of one of the troops getting onto the plane. You can just get a hint of how much gear is strapped to them. They have so much stuff on that they can barely walk on their own, and what you can't see is the two troops below him that have to push on his butt to hoist him up into the doorway:
http://www.dday-overlord.com/img/bob/film/imgfilm/band_of_brothers_c47_parachutistes_americain.jpg

Note that Bigby won't need the helmet and guns. But he's wearing as much equipment (all inside of packs) as you can physically draw on him.

Non Narration Cap: Three days later…

Ulmore: We shouldn't need anything but gravity to do the trick.

Cinderella: Are you ready to go, Bigby? Got all your equipment?

Humberjon: The hole's dug, sir.

Panel Three

Closer on Bigby and Cindy in Ulmore's palm. But in the background we can also see Humberjon using both hands to lift himself out of the hole he's dug. Now we can really see the immensity of the amount of gear strapped to poor Bigby.

Humberjon: I almost slipped through myself.

Bigby: I hope so. There's no room for anything else.

Panel Four

Ulmore holds his palm over the hole in the clouds and Bigby hops off of it and immediately starts falling towards the open hole. With all that gear, Bigby can barely give a small hop off of Ulmore's palm. He's still holding the musette bag in his arms.

Bigby: Better hold your hand directly over the hole, Ulmore. I can't jump far under all this weight.

Cindy: Be careless down there!

Page Thirteen (five panels)

Panel One

Now we switch scenes to the underside of the cloud layer. Dropping like a stone, Bigby comes hurtling out of the clouds into the open sky below, almost puncturing a hole in the clouds, trailing cloud vapor in his wake. He's still holding the musette bag in his arms. Oddly enough, though it was daytime up in the Cloud Kingdom, it's nighttime under the clouds in this new sky.

Cap (mission text): Stage Two: Insertion.

Cap (mission text): You will parachute into the Empire district of Calabri Anagni.

Panel Three

Still dropping towards the land far, far below, Bigby releases his musette bag which drops below him, the long straps (connecting the bag to his gear) trailing between them.

Cap (mission text): Be sure to pick a wilderness location for your drop zone.

Panel Four

The musette bag reaches the end of its two straps and snaps taut between the bag and Bigby above it.

Cap (mission text): And drop at night to avoid detection.

Panel Five

Closer on the still-plummeting Bigby, as he reaches for the rip-cord handle strapped to his chest and pulls it hard.

No captions or dialogue in this panel.

Page Fourteen (six panels)

Panel One

This isn't really a panel. It's the space you need to leave at the top of this page for the chapter title.

Title (display lettering): Chapter Three: Behind Enemy Lines

Panel Two

Now Bigby's chute has deployed and Bigby drifts down to the land below, the musette bag hanging about ten to twelve feet below him.

No captions or dialogue in this panel.

Panel Three

We switch our angle of view so that we can look down to see the land far below Bigby. Directly below him we can see Bigby headed for a hilly, forested area. Off in the not too far distance we can see the imperial city. Bigby will be coming down a few miles from Geppetto's hut and the magic grove of trees.

Cap (mission text): Pick a landing site close enough to your target area to be within a day's travel, making sure that you stay far away from the Imperial City.

Panel Four

Down in a very remote area of forest at night, the musette bag hits the forest floor hard, as Bigby drifts down nearly on top of it.

No caption or dialogue in this panel.

Panel Five

Now Bigby hits the earth (and rolls), narrowly avoiding the musette bag.

No caption or dialogue in this panel.

Panel Six

Just a few minutes later Bigby has un-strapped from all of his gear and is gathering up the limp parachute by rolling it up in his arms. His copious gear lies near him.

Cap (mission text): Immediately bury your expended chute and reserve chute pack. You won't be needing them any longer.

Cap (mission text): Inspect all remaining gear.

Page Fifteen (five panels)

Panel One

Now a bit later, still devoid of his gear, Bigby is kneeling over a small hole in the dirt he has dug with his hands, in order to plant a single magic bean in the hole. This is still in some remote part of the nighttime forest.

Cap (mission text): Plant your extraction bean in some remote location. Take note that it will take approximately twelve hours to fully deploy.

Panel Two

Now, about an hour later, Bigby, still in human form, is running lithely through the nighttime forest. He's wearing one backpack on his back and holding the big musette bag in his arms again.

Cap (mission text): Travel only at night.

Panel Three

Now in another part of the forest, we see Bigby hiding behind some rocks or trees as a trio of armored goblin soldiers pass by on a forest path. They are very close to Bigby but have no idea he's there. It's still nighttime.

Cap (mission text): Avoid all enemy contact.

Panel Four

Now it's daytime. We see Bigby lurking in the trees, looking down out of the forest towards Geppetto's hut and the grove of trees surrounding it. Maybe we can see Geppetto puttering around in his front yard, but this isn't vital.

Cap (mission text): If you arrive at the target site during daylight hours, wait until late the next night to begin operations.

Panel Five

It's nighttime again. Now we switch scenes to a shot of Bigby coming silent out of the woods, approaching a guard who is on foot, patrolling the area of Geppetto's hut and the magic grove of trees. Bigby is still in human form but has no packs on now. The guard isn't a goblin but is a human guard. Remember that Geppetto doesn't like the so-called lower races around his home? The guard has no idea Bigby's coming up behind him.

Cap (mission text): Stage Three: Preliminary Objectives.

Cap (mission text): First remove all guards from the area.

Page Sixteen (four panels)

Panel One

With a single deadly move, using only his bare hands, Bigby twists the guard's neck, breaking it instantly. In fact he nearly rips the guard's head entirely off of his body. Make this scene as graphic as we can. I want to stress the animal brutality of Bigby, when he's doing dirty deeds.

Sfx (guard's neck breaking — not too loud please): - ckricck -

Panel Two

In another spot we see a naked Bigby in mid-transformation to his wolf form. His clothes and gear are around his feet.

No captions or dialogue in this panel.

Panel Three

A bit later, in another part of the nighttime grove of magic trees, Bigby, in giant wolf form now, leaps out at a trio of guards, who are just turning to notice the danger they are in.

Cap (mission text): It's vital that you kill swiftly and silently…

Panel Four

This is the same scene just a few seconds later. All three guards are under Bigby being ripped to shreds. Bigby, still in wolf form, stands over his kills with a blood-painted muzzle. His attention is on his kills below him. Note that there will be some overhang of the forest in this panel so that two more guards (about to be seen in the following panel) can leap down on Bigby, who is too distracted by the ones he is dealing with now.

Cap (mission text): …so that no alarm can be raised in the woodcarver's cabin.

Page Seventeen (three panels)

Panel One

Same scene but now two more guards leap down towards Bigby's unprotected back, with swords or long knives brandished to plunge right into his back by the weight of their fall. Bigby just has time to look up at them, but there seems no way for Bigby to avoid their attack.

Guard #1: Devil spawn!

Panel Two

The guards don't fall. Suddenly they're both suspended in midair halfway between the ledge they leapt off of and Bigby's back. The panic in their faces shows that they hadn't planned this. Bigby is still looking up at them, unconcerned about their predicament.

Guard # 1: What's this?

Guard # 2: Dire sorcery!

Bigby: Not at all, gentlemen.

Panel Three

Same scene from another angle. Bigby is done with the other three kills and now watches as the two invisibly-suspended guards now fall (mostly on their heads) down at Bigby's feet.

Bigby: It's just my son, guarding my back.

Bigby: You can drop them now, boy. I'm ready for them.

Page Eighteen (five panels)

Panel One

Now we see Bigby, dressed again and in human form again. He has picked up the larger musette bag from his pile of gear and is walking away from us, into the depths of the grove itself.

Cap (mission text): Next enter the grove of magic trees and prepare them with the Special Packages — spaced for maximum effect.

Panel Two

It's still the same nighttime. We switch scenes a bit to see a wide shot, establishing shot of the forest trail leading up towards Geppetto's hut, from the Imperial City in the valley below. Basically this is the same view as in the Homelands collection, page 177, except that now there's no wagon or gob lizard riders on the trail. Instead we see one very drunk Pinocchio staggering up the trail, coming home alone from a late night spent in the town below. He's so drunk he can barely walk upright and is holding a bottle of some liquor in one hand.

Cap (mission text): Stage Four: Primary Objectives.

Cap (mission text): When the grove is prepared you can enter the woodcarver's hut.

Pinocchio (singing drunkenly): If the ocean were whiskey and I was a duck…

Panel Three

Closer on the drunken Pinocchio staggering up the night trail from the city below. Not that it's important, but this is the same drinking song Jack was singing when he came out of the Branstock Tavern in the March of the Wooden Soldiers story arc. I wonder if anyone will notice?

Pinocchio (singing drunkenly): I'd dive to the bottom and drink it all up.

Panel Four

From another angle we now see Pinocchio staggering up to the front door of Geppetto's cabin.

Pinocchio (drunkenly and quietly to himself): b — be very quiet now, Pin — Pinocchio.

Panel Five

Now we switch scenes to the inside of Geppetto's hut, specifically the workroom we saw so much of in the Homelands arc. There's no big cage in the center of the workroom now, but otherwise it looks much the same. It's very dark in here and we can't see Bigby at all. In the small light coming from the open doorway we can barely see Pinocchio. He is turning and making the shushing gesture with one finger to the wooden owl perched just inside the door.

Pinocchio (drunkenly and quietly): *Shhhhhhhhh*, Mr. Woody Owl. It's very important we don't wake my da — my da — don't wake the evil, bloody-handed Adversary.

Page Nineteen (three panels)

Panel One

Close on Pinocchio in the very dark room, striking a match with one hand and holding up a candle with the other.

Pinocchio (drunkenly and quietly): Kindly old conquerors need their sleep.

Panel Two

This is the big panel of the page. Except for the small panel above and the small panel below, it is nearly a splash page. In the foreground, facing away from us, Pinocchio has lit the candle. In the background we can see what Pinocchio sees: The work room is illuminated now and we see Bigby, in human form. Standing semi-crouched at the open closet door that contains the imprisoned Blue Fairy. He has turned away from the Blue Fairy and is making the same shushing gesture towards Pinocchio that he made towards the wooden owl. Pinocchio's body language shows us that he is quite surprised to see Bigby here.

Cap (mission text): If possible, try to free the Blue Fairy from her imprisonment. If that fails, try to destroy her.

Pinocchio (normal volume now): Bigby?

Bigby (quietly): *Shhhhhhh*, Pinocchio. Geppetto's sleeping only two rooms away and we don't want to wake him.

Panel Three

Closer on Pinocchio and Bigby at the open closet door showing the withered Blue Fairy in the closet. The surprise of discovering Bigby here seems to have sobered Pinocchio up some.

Pinocchio (quietly): What are you doing here, Bigby?

Bigby (quietly): Trying to murder your dad's power source. Didn't work, though.

Page Twenty (four panels)

Panel One

Another shot of Bigby and Pinocchio as Bigby quietly closes the door with the Blue Fairy inside it, a look of resignation on Bigby's face.

Pinocchio (quietly): The spells protecting her are nearly as complex as those protecting my dad.

Bigby (quietly): The very same conclusion I came to about twenty seconds ago.

Panel Two

Bigby turns to talk to Pinocchio, who looks deeply conflicted by what Bigby tells him.

Cap (mission text): Only if an opportunity presents itself, without jeopardizing the main mission, attempt to recruit Pinocchio into returning with you to Fabletown.

Bigby (quietly): I also came to get you, if you're ready to come home now.

Panel Three

Another shot of Bigby whispering to Pinocchio who looks like what he's saying is killing him to admit.

Cap (mission text): Our sorcerer's best theory is that his second transformation to flesh probably included the same loyalty bonds that infect all new puppet creations.

Pinocchio (quietly): How can I do that, Bigby?

Panel Four

Big panel. Wide shot. Suddenly the room gets brighter, as Geppetto appears in the other doorway — the one connecting this room to the rest of the cabin — holding a lantern up. Geppetto looks sleepy and is wearing his nightgown and slippers and nightcap.

Geppetto: My goodness.

Geppetto: What's going on in here?

Bigby: Geppetto!

Pinocchio: Oh no!

Page Twenty One (five panels)

Panel One

This isn't really a panel. It's the space you need to leave at the top of this page for the next chapter title.

Title (display lettering): Chapter Four: The Israel Analogy

Panel Two

With a sour and accusing look on his face, Geppetto steps further into the room with Bigby and Pinocchio.

Bigby: You might as well come on in, Geppetto. I'm ready for you now.

Geppetto: You're the Fabletown werewolf, aren't you?

Pinocchio: His name is Bigby, dad.

Panel Three

With the hand not holding the lantern, Geppetto points commandingly to the front door. Bigby looks relaxed and content to wait.

Geppetto: Pinocchio, son, go outside and summon the guards.

Bigby: Good luck with that. They're all dead.

Pinocchio: Be real careful, dad. Bigby's a stone cold killer.

Panel Four

Geppetto still looks pissed as he turns to accuse Bigby, who sits on the edge of one of the work tables, like an old friend who just popped in for a visit.

Geppetto: You won't be able to kill me. And my son is nearly as protected.

Pinocchio: I've still got years of spell treatments to catch up, but —

Bigby: Relax. You're both safe from me.

Panel Five

Closer on Bigby and Geppetto.

Bigby: I'm here to deliver a message from Fabletown.

Geppetto: Then say what you came to say and get out.

Bigby: Sure. How familiar are you with the Mundy world?

Page Twenty Two (five panels)

Panel One

Another shot of Bigby and Geppetto, who still looks cranky but also now looks a little confused as to what Bigby might be trying to get at.

Bigby: Ever hear of a country called Israel?

Geppetto: Who knows? Maybe. Why's that important?

Bigby: Here's what you need to know about it.

Panel Two

Bigby and Geppetto continue their adversarial conversation.

Bigby: Israel is a tiny country, surrounded on all sides by much larger countries dedicated to its eventual total destruction.

Geppetto: And why should that concern me?

Panel Three

Closer on Bigby. His expression shows that he admires the country he's talking about.

Bigby: Because they stay alive by being a bunch of tough little bastards who make the other guys pay dearly, every time they do anything against Israel.

Bigby: Some in the wider world constantly wail and moan about the endless cycle of violence and reprisal.

Panel Four

Another shot of Bigby telling his tale.

Bigby: But, since the alternative is non-existence, the Israelis seem determined to keep at it.

Bigby: They have a lot of grit and iron. I'm a big fan of them.

Panel Five

We pull back for another two-shot of Bigby and Geppetto, who is getting tired of the speech. Geppetto shows no fear in Bigby's presence. He entirely trusts the spells protecting him.

Geppetto: Are you near to being done? I'd like to go back to sleep.

Bigby: Here's the part that concerns you. Fabletown has decided to adopt the Israel template in whole.

Bigby: You've no doubt guessed that you guys play the part of the vast powers arrayed against us.

Page Twenty Three (five panels)

Panel One

Now we close in on Bigby and his look is deadly serious.

Bigby: Every time you hurt us we're going to damage you much worse in return.

Bigby: It will always happen. Always. You're the only one who can end the cycle.

Panel Two

Now Bigby smiles a small, sly, predator's smile.

Bigby: And keep this in mind. You have a huge empire to protect.

Bigby: Guard the ten million most likely targets and there will still be a hundred million ripe, unprotected targets we can hit.

Panel Three

We widen out to another group shot. Since it's been awhile since we've seen Pinocchio, let's include him in this shot too. Bigby is reaching into one of the oversized pockets in his shorts.

Geppetto: Okay, I understand now. I'll ponder your threat.

Bigby: Not so fast, old gaffer. Accounts aren't balanced yet. You still have the wooden soldier raid against Fabletown to pay for.

Panel Four

Closer on Bigby and Geppetto. Bigby has pulled a small radio transmitter (the kind used to set off bombs) out of his pocket and holds it up for Geppetto to see.

Geppetto: But you already know you can't hurt us.

Bigby: Think so? I'm about to stick it to you where it hurts most. See this? It's Mundy magic, which they call high-tech. It's a radio transmitter.

Panel Five

With a smile, Bigby pushes the red button on the face of the small transmitter.

Bigby: It's about to talk to another bunch of Mundy magic called plastic explosive, formed into about three dozen bombs strapped to tree trunks.

Bigby: This would be a good time to duck, because when I push this little red button —

Page Twenty Four (one panel)

Panel One

This is a full-page splash. We move our view to the exterior of the woodcarver's hut, with a wide enough shot to take in as much of the magic grove as you can show us. All at once the entire grove goes up in a series of explosions. The blasts aren't directed at the cabin, but the cabin is too close to escape all damage. The entire grove goes up in massive blasts that already show the fires to come.

No captions or dialogue in this panel. No sound effects either. We can have the art tell the entire story on this page.

Page Twenty Five (five panels)

Panel One

It's about an hour later. Morning has just begun. This is another exterior shot of the same area shown in the previous panel. What little remains of the magic grove is still on fire. The cabin has suffered considerable damage and is also starting to burn.

Non Narration Cap: Sometime later…

Voice (from cabin): Come on, old man. Your cabin's started to burn.

Panel Two

Closer on the sagging front door of the cabin, Bigby comes out, literally carrying Geppetto under one arm and Pinocchio under the other.

Bigby: And even if those spells protect you from burning up with it, I doubt you'll want to wait for them to find you two under the scorched remains.

Geppetto: *cough — cough!*

Panel Three

Bigby unceremoniously dumps the two on the ground, a safe ways away from the fire. All characters are covered with dust and ash from the explosions.

Bigby: I've just taken your magic grove away from you.

Bigby: Yeah, I know it'll grow back — eventually — but I suspect it'll be at least a generation before you can produce new wooden children from it.

Panel Four

As Pinocchio and Geppetto begin to sit up, Bigby bends down to speak his final words to them.

Bigby: That's your punishment for invading Fabletown. See how we did much worse to you than what you did to us?

Bigby: Do yourself a big favor and learn the lesson here.

Panel Five

In our final panel of this scene, Pinocchio and Geppetto, still a bit dazed from their ordeal, are in the foreground, beginning to pick themselves up off the rough ground. In the background Bigby is walking away from them, towards the nearest unburned woods.

Bigby: That was the stick, now here's the carrot. Most of the heads from your invasion force are still alive.

Bigby: We might be willing to exchange them for things we want — if you can convince us you're inclined to be nice from now on.

Page Twenty Six (five panels)

Panel One

It's later in that same day. Bigby is in wolf form, running through the deep woods as fast as he can. Make sure we can see he's carrying his shorts in his mouth.

Cap (mission text): Stage Five: Extraction.

Cap (mission text): After completion of all objectives, return to the extraction point as quickly as possible, no matter the time of day.

Panel Two

Bigby is at his extraction point — the spot where he planted the magic bean several pages ago. He's back in human form and wearing the pair of shorts he brought back with him. Now a huge beanstalk has grown in the same spot. It's as big as the one growing up from the Farm at the beginning of the issue. Bigby is crouching at the base of the beanstalk, attaching another set of plastic explosive bombs to the base of the stalk. He's placing them so that the leaves or something will conceal them, when he's done placing them. Make sure we can see the remaining backpack here where the remaining bombs were stashed.

Cap (mission text): The beanstalk should have fully deployed by the time you reach it. Plant the remaining bombs at its base in places of concealment…

Panel Three

Naked except for his shorts, Bigby is now high above the forest, climbing up the beanstalk towards the sky. Down below him we can see goblin troops climbing after him.

Cap (mission text): …to avoid detection from any forces that might give chase.

Panel Four

Now we see a closer look at all of the goblin and other Empire forces climbing up after Bigby. At least one of the enemy troops needs to be a human-looking captain.

Guard Captain: Climb faster, you filthy gobs, or the Emperor will kill every bloody one of you!

Panel Five

Bigby is near the top, climbing up to just below cloud level. With one hand he's holding out the radio transmitter. With the other hand he's reaching for the end of a rope that's dropping down from the clouds above, paralleling the beanstalk.

Cap (mission text): Be sure to activate the radio detonator while still in the Empire dimension, to ensure a good signal.

Page Twenty Seven (five panels)

Panel One

Down at the base of the beanstalk, we see more explosions go off, blasting the base of the beanstalk to smithereens.

No captions or dialogue in this panel.

Panel Two

Midway up the beanstalk we can see the beanstalk buckling and toppling, and the various goblins and other troops falling to their certain deaths far below.

Goblin Troop: Imperial approved gods and demons save us!

Panel Three

Back up at the underside of the clouds, Bigby is hanging from the bottom of the rope, looking down and smiling. No part of the beanstalk shows any longer.

Cap (mission text): Your final ascent will be up the secondary escape line.

Panel Four

Same scene, but now Bigby is disappearing into the cloud layer as he climbs, hand over hand, up the rope.

Cap (mission text): Don't forget to grab it before destroying the beanstalk.

Panel Five

Same scene. Now Bigby is gone and all that remains is the end of the rope, dangling out of the cloud layer.

Cap (mission text): End of mission briefing. Good luck and be careful, Bigby.

Page Twenty Eight (four panels)

Panel One

This isn't a real panel. It's the space you need to leave at the top of this page for the next chapter title.

Title (display lettering): Chapter Five: Home is the Hunter

Panel Two

We switch scenes to an establishing shot of New York City in the summer daytime.

Non Narration Cap: Two weeks later.

Voice (from city): Bigby!

Same Voice (connected balloon): Welcome back!

Panel Three

Now we move down into the city to see an exterior establishing shot of the Woodland Building in Fabletown.

Non Narration Cap: In Fabletown.

Voice (from Woodland Building): Hail the conquering hero!

Same Voice (connected balloon): If I had any confidence I'd survive it, I'd give you a big hug right now.

Panel Four

Big panel. We move inside to the Woodland's lobby to see the following characters gathered there: Bigby; Fly; Prince Charming; Beast; Beauty and Grimble. Everyone is crowding around Bigby, delighted to see him. A celebratory mood infects them all. Bigby and Charming are shaking hands. Fly stands off a bit but looks like he's about to explode with joy. Bigby is back to being dressed in his trademark brown rumpled suit. Fly is dressed as always. Charming is dressed and coifed perfectly in his best suit — not a hair out of place. Beast is dressed as usual. Beauty is dressed well in her standard bright colors. Grimble is in human form in his security guard uniform.

Charming: I just finished reading your after-action report and it's marvelous! One hundred percent success!

Bigby: I hate to admit it, Mr. Mayor, but you crafted a good plan.

Beast: Well done, sheriff!

Bigby: Not my name anymore, Beast. That's your headache from now on.

Beauty: So you aren't coming back to your old job?

Page Twenty Nine (four panels)

Panel One

The scene continues. Bigby is answering Beauty's question, but he doesn't look her way. Instead he gives Prince Charming a very serious look in the eye — one that says: I did what I agreed to do, so pay me what you promised. Charming's expression shows that he fully gets Bigby's meaning.

Bigby: Nope. I'm retired.

Bigby: For good.

Charming: Ah, yes — well, perhaps it's time we discussed the details of the retirement package I promised.

Panel Two

Suddenly Flycatcher can't hold back any longer. He leaps forward and throws a massive hug on Bigby that takes everyone — Bigby most of all — by surprise.

Flycatcher: I can't believe you're really here, Bigby!

Bigby: Woah!

Panel Three

Bigby carefully disengages from the unexpected hug — he doesn't do hugs and he's embarrassed by being caught in one. Fly also looks a bit embarrassed by his emotional outburst and now can't make eye contact with Bigby. The others try to look like they didn't notice anything untoward just happened — like an elevator full of old world aristocrats trying to pretend that no one just farted.

Bigby: Uhm… Nice to see you too, Fly.

Flycatcher (quietly): Uh, yeah… I guess what I meant to say was… uhm, I really missed you and welcome home.

Panel Four

Now Charming steps forward, breaking the spell of communal embarrassment. He lightly takes Bigby by one arm and deftly maneuvers him out of the cluster of people, moving him back towards the stairs to the Business Office.

Charming: Sentiments we all share, Flycatcher.

Charming: Now, if you'll excuse us, Bigby and I have a bit of private business to resolve.

Page Thirty (five panels)

Panel One

We switch scenes to a long-distance establishing shot of the Farm in upstate New York. It's daytime on a sunny day, several days later than the previous page.

Non Narration Cap: Several days later, at Fabletown's Farm annex in Upstate New York.

Panel Two

We move down to see a wide-shot view, looking down on a beat-up old Range Rover type passenger truck slowly bouncing over the uneven terrain of the wilder lands surrounding the Farm. This is the grassy area leading out to the hilly Valley of the Big Sleepers, as seen in the Animal Farm story arc.

Voice (from truck): Okay, will you please tell me now where we're going?

Same Voice (connected balloon): I don't understand what the big secret's all about.

Panel Three

Closer on the Range Rover, as it pulls up at an obstacle too big to maneuver over.

Voice (from driver's side of truck): Relax, sister. It's a surprise.

Same Voice (connected balloon): And we're here. At least we're as far as we can get by truck.

Panel Four

This is nearly the same scene as the previous panel, except now both front doors open and Snow White gets out on the passenger side, and Rose Red gets out on the driver's side. Snow White is dressed in a summer dress (no pants, please) and wearing her hair loose. She doesn't have the kind of shoes one should wear for tramping about in the wilderness. Snow pulls her cane out with her. Rose is dressed more practically.

Rose Red: We walk from here — or to be more precise, *you* do.

Rose Red: I wish you'd dressed better, Snow.

Snow: Sorry, but when I chose my ensemble this morning, I didn't realize you'd be kidnapping me for a wilderness adventure.

Panel Five

Snow gives Rose Red a questioning look as Rose Red points away from the car, towards the forested hills in the distance — pointing towards the hills surrounding the Valley of the Big Sleepers.

Snow: And what do you mean? I walk alone from here?

Rose Red: Head that way, sis. I'll be waiting here when you're ready to come back.

Page Thirty One (six panels)

Panel One

This isn't really a panel. It's the space you need to leave at the top of the page for the next chapter title.

Title (display lettering): Chapter Six: Restoration

Panel Two

In the foreground, using her cane to help her, Snow starts walking towards (us) the Valley of the Big Sleepers. Pretty far in the background — not so far that they couldn't still hear each other — Rose Red sits on the hood of the Range Rover, watching Snow walk away from her. Snow looks back at Rose Red as she walks.

Snow: If this is another of your pranks, Rose Red, I swear I'll —

Rose Red: Keep walking, Snow. All mysteries will soon be made clear.

Panel Three

Now we see the first of three nearly identical panels. In the foreground we see the full figure of Snow White, walking away from us, towards the background. She's walking through the hilly tall grass, headed towards the tree line of the forest that begins just before the terrain starts rising up into the hills surrounding the Valley of the Big Sleepers. In this panel it can barely be seen, but just before the trees begin we can just begin to see the tiny shape of a person sitting on a big rock, just this side of the tree line. Snow is walking towards this figure.

Snow: Huh?

Panel Three

Now in this second of the three nearly identical panels, Snow is still walking towards the figure which is a bit closer to us now and we're just beginning to make out some of the details of him. Do you know who he is?

Snow: Is that - ?

Panel Four

Now in this third of the three nearly identical panels, Snow is much closer to the figure, and can now tell who it is. We are just close enough to see that it's Bigby, in his standard rumpled brown suit and trench coat, sitting quietly on the rock, waiting for Snow to get there. Even facing away from us, Snow's body language tells us she's finally recognized who it is.

Snow: Oh no —

Panel Five

Close-up of Snow's excited face as she recognizes who it is in front of her. Her face lights up like the sun breaking through storm clouds for the first time in a year.

Snow: Oh my God!

Page Thirty Two (five panels)

Panel One

Snow tosses her cane aside and starts running through the grass, a look of complete joy on her face.

Snow: Bigby!

Panel Two

Snow has reached Bigby who has stood up from his makeshift seat just in time for her to throw herself into his arms, burying her face in his chest. He smiles at her reaction to seeing him.

Bigby (quietly): Hello, Snow.

Snow (yelling): You came back! You're here! You - !

Panel Three

Just as suddenly Snow backs out of the embrace, pushing herself away at arm's length so she can look up at him. There is a look of concern (approaching near-panic) on her face. His quiet, confident smile is still in place though.

Snow: Oh no! You're not allowed to —

Snow: You have to go! Right now!

Snow: If they catch you on the Farm they'll kill you!

Panel Four

Bigby playfully places a few fingers on Snow's mouth to stop her from talking. Her eyes are still wide with concern.

Bigby: Settle down, Snow. You're babbling.

Snow: But —

Bigby: I know I'm not allowed on the Farm, but this isn't the Farm.

Panel Five

Snow stands back from Bigby now. She's still upset, or distraught, but Bigby refuses to look anything but happy and far too sure of himself.

Snow: Of course it is!

Bigby: Not any longer. From now on the Farm ends where Rose Red dropped you off. This area belongs to me now — or us, if you like.

Page Thirty Three (four panels)

Panel One

Wider shot. Bigby gently takes Snow by one arm and starts to guide her towards the hills leading up to the Valley of the Big Sleepers.

Snow: I don't understand.

Bigby: I bought this land from Fabletown, in return for ending a war — or maybe starting one. I guess we'll see.

Bigby: Come on. Take a walk with me. I want to show you a thing or two.

Panel Two

Closer on Snow and Bigby as she suddenly stops walking and turns to face him again. Now there is a look of quiet desperation on her face. Tears are beading her eyes and she clutches Bigby's arms hard.

Snow: Wait!

Snow: There's something I need to —

Snow: Bigby, did our son find you?

Panel Three

We pull back again. As Bigby turns and gestures to one side of him, as if he's about to introduce someone, but there's nothing but empty air where Bigby is looking. Snow looks simultaneously confused and scared and hopeful (I have no idea what that would look like, but I have every confidence you can pull it off).

Bigby: Of course.

Bigby: Ghost, give your mother a kiss.

Panel Four

This is a full figure shot of Snow as she's rocked back on her feet by some invisible force (not far enough that she's in danger of falling over, but enough that we can tell some physical force just collided with her). Her hair and the skirt of her summer dress are being blown all over (sort of like Marilyn Monroe's famous wind-blown skirt scene in whichever of her movies that's from), even though the grass all around her is unaffected by any wind. Snow's eyes are very wide now, and her mouth looks like she's just been surprised by a stolen kiss from someone or something she can't see. Bigby stands a bit apart from her, grinning like the cat that ate the canary.

Sfx (gust of wind — not too big, please): Wuff!

Snow: !

Page Thirty Four (five panels)

Panel One

Another shot of basically the same scene, but now the gust of wind is gone. Snow is standing there quivering with emotion, with tears streaming down her face.

Puff (word balloon with no pointer): Mommy's crying. Why's she crying, Daddy? Did I upset her again?

Bigby: Don't worry, son. Those are happy tears, not sad ones.

Panel Two

Closer on Snow's happy face, with tears streaming unchecked down her face, but we can also see some of Bigby in this shot.

Snow (barely able to talk): You named him Ghost?

Bigby: Seemed to fit.

Panel Three

Bigby reaches out and takes Snow, softly, by the hand.

Bigby: He'll be safe here. He's learned how to keep his existence secret. You and I are the only living creatures who know about him.

Bigby: We'll have to decide when to introduce him to his brothers and sisters.

Panel Four

Arm in arm, Bigby turns them to start walking towards the hills again, but Snow turns her face back towards the direction in which she dropped her cane.

Bigby: So now, like I said, let's the three of us go for a walk.

Snow: Hold on, I need to go back and get my cane.

Panel Five

Without going back for her cane, Bigby continues leading Snow away from us.

Bigby: No, you won't need it.

Bigby: You can lean on me from now on.

Page Thirty Five (six panels)

Panel One

This isn't really a panel. It's the space you need to leave at the top of the page for the next chapter title.

Title (display lettering): Chapter 7: The Big Valley

Panel Two

It's a little later in the day. We see a wide shot long shot view of the Valley of the Big Sleepers, as first seen in the Animal Farm story arc, and the hills surrounding it. Snow and Bigby are on top of one of the hills, looking down into the secluded valley, but we're too far away from them in this shot to see them. We want to see how big and sprawling the valley is, now that it isn't filled with sleeping giants.

Voice (from closest hilltop): The Valley of the Big Sleepers couldn't be used for anything as long as it was filled up with sleeping giants and dragons.

Same Voice (connected balloon): But it's empty now and pretty roomy as it turns out. Lots of untouched forest.

Panel Three

Now we slowly pan in closer. We can just begin to make out Bigby and Snow, standing together on the nearest hilltop, her arm in his, looking down (away from us) into the big valley.

Bigby: Which means the dilemma keeping us apart no longer applies.

Bigby (connected balloon): I wasn't allowed to ever visit the Farm, and because of the nature of the children, you weren't allowed to live anywhere but the Farm.

Panel Four

Now we pan in even closer to Bigby and Snow, looking down into the valley. Snow turns to face Bigby.

Bigby: But you can live here, and now that it's officially separate from the Farm, so can I.

Snow: Not so fast, Bigby. Since we're in this area, I want you to accompany me to one of the caves. There's something you need to see.

Panel Five

Close enough on them to see that Snow's looking around her and Bigby, trying to guess where their invisible son is. Bigby looks surprised by what the son tells her.

Snow: Uh… Ghost? Can you wait here for a little while? Mommy and Daddy need to go do something just for grownups, but we'll be right back, okay?

Puff (floating word balloon with no pointer): Is it lovey stuff? Daddy always made me leave the cabin when he wanted to do lovey stuff with the Sarah lady.

Panel Six

Silent panel. Snow gives Bigby a killer (not in the good way) look. Her cheeks flush red with anger (color note). Bigby has the good grace to look embarrassed and maybe even a little ashamed.

No captions or dialogue in this panel.

Page Thirty Six (five panels)

Panel One

Same panel, but now Snow is very visibly keeping herself under control and is just able to speak again.

Snow: Okay, that's a conversation we need to have real soon.

Snow: But first things first.

Panel Two

We switch scenes to the outside (looking at the entrance) of one of the many caves in these hills. This isn't one of the caves we've seen before. It's still daytime of the same day.

Voice (from cave): Since there are so many natural caves in these hills, I decided to use one to keep certain things hidden.

Panel Three

Now we move in to see the interior of this small and cozy cave. There are at least three cardboard boxes of stuff here. Plus a portable folding chair and a wooden box being used as a makeshift table. A gas camping-style lantern sits on the table, but it isn't lit. There's enough light coming in from the cave entrance. Snow has picked up the smallest of the cardboard boxes — at least as big as a shoe box, but maybe even a bit bigger — and is holding it out to Bigby. Snow is all business now, just like she used to be back when she was running Fabletown.

Snow: You have some work to do before I can let you see the kids — our other kids.

Snow: First some reading. This box is full of all of the letters they wrote you. Each one has a copy of your reply paper-clipped to it.

Panel Four

Snow points then to a much bigger cardboard box on the cave floor which is open at the top and is full of all sorts of wrapped gifts.

Snow: Then you can unwrap all of the gifts they sent you for Christmas, birthdays and Father's Day.

Snow: Make damn sure you memorize who gave you what.

Panel Five

Out of another box, Snow picks up a fat photo album and hands it, open at some random page, to Bigby.

Snow: And finally we'll go over the gifts you sent them, so it doesn't come as a complete surprise to you when they mention them.

Bigby: Got it.

Page Thirty Seven (five panels)

Panel One

We switch scenes yet again to Snow and Bigby walking towards us this time, strolling slowly together now like two old friends out for a summer's walk. Sometime between pages Bigby has retrieved Snow's cane, which he carries for her, midway down the shaft, as if it's just some stick he picked up along the trail.

Bigby: We can talk about her in detail if you like, but the gist is this.

Bigby: Sarah's one of the ways I tried to forget you. I also tried booze and solitude.

Bigby: Nothing worked. How could it?

Panel Two

They pause and he turns to look at her. They both know this is the most serious moment in their lives.

Bigby: So here it is, one last time and then I'll leave you alone forever, if that's what you decide.

Bigby: I love you, Snow, and have since the hour we first met.

Panel Three

He drops the cane and takes her by each of her arms, but not too close, so that they can still look at each other. She's like a cornered doe, almost quivering with fear.

Bigby: Hell, I wanted you even before then. Since before we existed.

Bigby: As if every movement of every star and planet, every tick of creation's clock occurred only so that we could someday find each other.

Snow: Bigby, I —

Panel Four

We move in just a wee bit closer on them. We can see that Bigby is scared too. For the first time in his very long existence he's finally and completely vulnerable — putting everything on the line.

Bigby: I'm certainly no handsome prince, come to steal you away from all the cares of the world. I can never offer you riches and palaces or any sort of luxury.

Bigby: But I'd think you've had your fill of such things by now.

Panel Five

We move in just a wee bit closer on them. He grips her a bit tighter.

Bigby: What I can offer you is a home in our valley, where we can raise our kids.

Bigby: And I'm old-fashioned enough that I think we should be married to do it.

Page Thirty Eight (five panels)

Panel One

Silent panel. They're still looking directly at each other. Snow looks scared, like she may turn and run at any second.

No captions or dialogue in this panel.

Panel Two

Same scene, but now a very small smile steals over Bigby's face.

Bigby: I think that's your cue to say something now.

Panel Three

Same scene, but now Snow moves one hand up behind Bigby's neck. She's surrendered now and it shows as an almost supernatural calm that has settled over her.

Snow (very quietly): okay.

Snow (very quietly): you've defeated me.

Panel Four

Same scene. Snow slowly pulls Bigby's head down for a kiss, even as she raises her own head up towards his.

Snow (very quietly): you win.

Panel Five

Same scene. They kiss. This is the truest of true love's kisses since the beginning of time. It's every poem ever written and every song ever sung. This is the one panel at which the dream of every female reader of FABLES has come true. Each and every one of them must be made to cry or squeal or swoon like a character in a Jane Austen novel. Don't blow it, Buckingham. We sort of, kind of know where you live.

No captions or dialogue in this panel.

Page Thirty Nine (four panels)

Panel One

This isn't really a panel. It's the space you need to leave at the top of the page for the next chapter title.

Title (display lettering): Chapter 8: The Wedding

Panel Two

We switch scenes to an exterior establishing shot of the City of Baghdad — the fantastical one in the Homelands, first seen in The Arabian Nights (and Days) story arc.

Lettering Note: Todd: From now on, for the rest of this issue, we have some standard narration captions. No special font or script style, please.

Cap: Things moved pretty quickly then.

Voice (from city): King Cole! King Cole! An urgent message for you, Excellency!

Panel Two

Down in one of the bustling Baghdad streets, King Cole has just been handed a message on a sheet of parchment. He holds it in both hands, eyes wide with absolute surprise. He couldn't tear his eyes off the page if a horde of all-girl Nazi death zombies were bearing down on him (note that there are no death zombies bearing down on him). He can't believe what he's reading. The Arabian servant/messenger stands near him, dutifully waiting for his instructions. Cole is dressed pretty much as he was when we last saw him.

King Cole: Oh my dear Lord!

King Cole: Run quickly and find Sinbad, or one of the other city leaders! I must travel back to the Mundy world as soon as possible!

King Cole: They can't do this without me!

Panel Three

This is the big panel of the page. Snow's kids, all in good clothes and all in human form, have been driven out (in the same Range Rover Rose was driving earlier) to the spot just over the new official border of the Farm, to where Bigby is waiting to meet them. On one side of the panel the kids are clustered around the Range Rover and around Rose Red, suddenly overcome with group shyness and reluctant to approach the scary man before them. On the other side of the panel, Bigby stands, trying not to look scary, calmly waiting for one of them to work his courage up to approach him. Snow stands in the center, trying to coax the kids to get over their fears. Note that Snow and Rose Red will be dressed differently than when we last saw them, to indicate days have passed. Bigby will still be dressed in his standard rumpled suit and open trench coat. Note also that Bigby still looks as scruffy as ever, but hasn't been smoking since he got back. He doesn't need to out in the remote Farm area.

Cap: Days seemed to blur together.

Snow: How can every single one of you ruffians possibly be shy all of a sudden? You've seen his pictures and read his letters.

Snow: Come and meet your father.

Page Forty (five panels)

Panel One

We switch scenes to another day, when Snow and Rose Red are sitting together on the steps in front of the main house of the Farm. Once again they're dressed differently than when we last saw them. Both women have obviously been crying like babies.

Cap: Plans were made.

Rose Red: What I have to say is simply this.

Rose Red: If you pick anyone else as your Maid of Honor, forget free babysitting forever.

Panel Two

Now we switch to another overhead (looking down) shot of the area where the Farm ends and Bigby's new lands begin. An entire caravan of trucks have pulled up there, loaded with cut lumber and all sorts of building supplies — everything one would need to build a mostly modern house out in the middle of nowhere. We can see the tiny figures of Boy Blue and Flycatcher, both dressed in work clothes. They've just gotten out of the lead truck as the equally tiny figure of Reynard the Fox has approached them from across the grassy field.

Boy Blue: Reynard! Finally! Where are the trolls?

Reynard: Relax. They're on the way. They don't move as fast as I do. But they're sturdy. Each one can pack a ton.

Panel Three

We move down closer to Boy Blue and Reynard and Fly, as Fly consults a clip board he's holding in his hands. Boy Blue points to the hills surrounding the former Valley of the Big Sleepers and which will probably be renamed Wolf Valley from now on. Blue is in a hard hat. He looks every bit the construction foreman.

Boy Blue: Good, because this is as far as the trucks will go and we need to get all of this heavy stuff over those hills.

Fly: I've put up notices for every carpenter, plumber, brick-layer and stone mason in Fabletown.

Panel Four

Closer on Blue.

Boy Blue: Get them all out here by yesterday, Fly.

Boy Blue: I'm determined to have their house finished by the time they get back from their honeymoon.

Panel Five

We see a commercial jet airliner in the air over the ocean.

Voice (from jet): I'm in the air now, maybe six hours out. Whatever you do, don't let them start without me!

Page Forty One (four panels)

Panel One

We see an exterior shot of the Woodland Building at night, early enough that most of the lights are still on.

Cap: Things got hectic, as things will.

Voice (from the Woodland): My father was living at the Farm? Raising my kids?

Same Voice (connected balloon): And they're afraid of letting *me* out there? Don't they recognize a *real* monster when they see one?

Panel Two

We switch scenes to the interior of Frau Totenkinder's apartment, where Sheriff Beast is sitting in the living room enjoying a cup of tea, while she tends to her knitting.

Totenkinder: So the wolf and the princess and all seven children will live out in the woods?

Beast: Six kids, Frau Totenkinder, not seven.

Totenkinder: Oh yes, six. At my age it's so hard to remember things.

Panel Three

We switch scenes to the inside of the Business Office, where Beauty and Prince Charming and Bufkin are getting some work done. Bufkin needs to be seen so that Beauty keeps her pledge never to be alone in a room with Charming again. As they work, they talk. Please don't make them look like they're actively having an argument. This is just normal everyday sniping at each other while the work gets done.

Beauty: So just like that, Bigby and Snow get an entire valley all to themselves?

Charming: They earned it. When you've served Fabletown for a few centuries, we'll worry about what you've earned.

Panel Four

It's daytime and Snow White is back for a visit. She's walking across Bullfinch Street surrounded by a flock of people trying to show her dress patterns, and seating charts and so on. The crowd includes one obvious butcher, one obvious baker and one obvious candlestick maker trailing behind her. I'd like to do this visually, without identifying the butcher, baker and candlestick maker by words. I think the small joke will work better if the readers can figure it out for themselves, but that just puts more pressure on you to make them look like nothing else than who they are.

Butcher: Prime rib! Pork roasts! Such a feast I'm going to prepare for you!

Baker: And a wedding cake twenty layers high!

Candlestick Maker: A thousand candles is my gift, to match the stars we dine under!

Page Forty Two (six panels)

Mark: I know this page will be crowded. I've asked for a lot in these six panels, but I want the page to look crowded — as if pressure is building up just before the big wedding.

Panel One

We switch scenes to the Woodland lobby at night as a breathless King Cole comes rushing in from the outside door, worried that he's not in time for the big event. Grimble is behind the security counter, with his feet up on the desk. He calmly lifts his cap to look at King Cole. Grimble doesn't look surprised, as if King Cole arriving from the Homelands is something that happens all the time.

Cole: Have I arrived in time? Am I too late?

Grimble: For what?

Grimble (connected balloon): Hey, did you know there's a big wedding day after tomorrow?

Panel Two

Flycatcher and Red Riding Hood are strolling down Bullfinch Street in the evening. She has no idea who Fly is talking about. She doesn't know Bigby is the Big Bad Wolf.

Fly: And please don't be frightened when you see Bigby Wolf. He's really a nice guy now. Honest.

Riding Hood: Why would I be frightened of a man I've never met before?

Panel Three

It's the next day and we are out in the Valley of the Big Sleepers (Wolf Valley) where, in the background, all sorts of Fables are working on building Snow and Bigby's dream house. Construction has just started. There are piles of lumber and a cement mixer and just the first frames of the house-to-come going up. Blue is back there leading the workers, but we don't need to see him. In the foreground, Prince Charming has arrived to look at the construction progress. He's in a suit, but wearing a hard hat, even though he's not anywhere near the construction. He wears a hard hat because that's what businessmen do when they visit job sites: they want to look like they have something to do with the progress being made. Reynard is at Charming's feet, also observing the work, but right now he's looking up at Charming, with a sour look on his face (on his muzzle?).

Reynard: I'll never forgive you, Prince Charming.

Charming: What? Did I do something to you?

Reynard: It's what you didn't do. You didn't keep your promise to provide all the animal Farm Fables with permanent transformations.

Panel Four

Same scene, but now Charming looks down at Reynard with a quizzical look on his face.

Reynard: If you had, I could have become a man, like Bigby did. And I would've had more than enough time to win Snow, while he was away.

Charming: Who are you again? Do we even know each other?

Panel Five

It's the day of the wedding. Somewhere Snow is dressing into her wedding dress, with Rose Red's help and talking to Rose. Snow has a softly frantic, worried expression on her face.

Snow: Am I doing the right thing?

Panel Six

It's the day of the wedding. Somewhere Bigby is getting into his tux, as Boy Blue helps him tie his tie. Bigby doesn't look at all comfortable about this.

Bigby: Am I about to make a big mistake?

Page Forty Three (five panels)

Once again, Mark, I think it might be tough getting all this in on this page, still leaving room for far too much dialogue, but it all suddenly opens up in the next page, which is the effect we're after.

Panel One

Finally it's time for the wedding. Once again we see the land bordering where the Farm leaves off and Bigby's (and Snow's) new land begins. We see all sorts of trucks and cars (the ones rugged enough to travel out this far off-road) sort of haphazardly parked in a big clump, where Rose Red's Range Rover was parked several pages ago. The Range Rover is there too. Beyond these cars we are looking at the grasslands leading to the forested lands beyond, and Wolf Valley beyond that.

Voice (from near the tree line, beyond the parked cars): Dearly Beloved.

Same Voice (connected balloon): We are gathered here together in the sight of God to join this man and this woman together in holy matrimony.

Panel Two

Just beyond the parked cars is a newly made — rather hastily made — sign that reads: Warning, you are leaving Farm territory. Beyond this sign we can see the far treeline.

Voice (from somewhere in the background): Which is an honorable estate, instituted by God in Heaven, into which these two present come now to be joined.

Panel Three

Now we move in to see one big tree, standing just a little ways apart from the far treeline has been decorated with bright ribbons and other decorations. All sorts of picnic tables have been set up to one side of the tree, and a largish wedding crowd is gathered to the other side of the tree. The wedding is taking place.

Voice (from wedding crowd): Therefore if any Fable can show just cause why they may not lawfully be joined together, let him speak now or else hereafter hold his peace.

Panel Four

Now we close in just enough on the wedding crowd to barely make out that King Cole is at the head of the group, performing the wedding, and Bigby and Snow are in their proper places. Please don't show too many details. We don't want to rob the readers of the big spread following this page. Is there some kind of decorative arch behind the dais where Cole is standing?

Voice: Wilt thou, Bigby Wolf, have this woman to be thy wedded wife, to live together after God's ordinance in the holy state of matrimony?

Same Voice (connected balloon): Wilt thou love her, comfort her, honor and keep her, in sickness and in health, forsaking all others and keep thee only unto her, so long as you both shall live?

Bigby: *Yes* — I mean, I will.

Panel Five

Same scene.

Voice: Wilt thou, Snow White, have this man to be thy wedded husband, to live together after God's ordinance in the holy state of matrimony?

Voice: Wilt thou obey him and serve him, love, honor and keep him in sickness and in health, and forsaking all others, keep thee only unto him, so long as you both shall live?

Snow: I will.

Pages Forty Four and Forty Five (one panel)

This is a double-page spread. Now we see the wedding scene in all its glory. In the foreground we see King Cole (facing away from us) conducting the wedding. In front of him are Snow White, with Rose Red next to her as her Maid of Honor, and Bigby Wolf, with Boy Blue next to him as his Best Man. In a wide semicircle arrayed behind them, from one side of the spread to the other, we see the wedding guests, and it's a big crowd. Basically we see every Fable in good standing in Fabletown and the Farm. We do not see Jack (missing) and Bluebeard and Trusty John (both dead) and such like them. Fill these pages with mostly happy (Reynard is here, but not quite happy). The kids are there all in human form and all dressed up. Mr. North isn't there. Red Riding Hood is standing near Fly and maybe looking daggers at the three hot Arabian Babes (last page of Arabian Nights and Days). Grimble is there standing next to Hakim, and so on. Charming, Beauty and Beast and Totenkinder should be there, of course. Who else should be there? Basically I want you to pack this scene in with as many characters as you can possibly draw. Snow and Bigby are turned towards each other, her hand in his, saying their vows.

Bigby: I take thee, Snow, to be my wedded wife, to have and to hold from this day forward, for better or worse, for richer or poorer, in sickness and in health, to love and to cherish, till death do us part, and thereunto I plight thee my troth.

Snow: I take thee, Bigby, to be my wedded husband to have and to hold from this day forward, for better or worse, for richer or poorer, in sickness and in health, to love and to cherish, till death do us part, and thereunto I plight thee my troth.

King Cole: Forasmuch as Bigby and Snow have consented together in holy wedlock and have witnessed the same before God and this company, I pronounce therefore that they be man and wife together.

Page Forty Six

Panel One

Now we see Bigby and Snow kiss, while behind them we see Cole, beaming with joy as he gives them permission to kiss.

King Cole: You may kiss the bride.

Panel Two

Later they all feast at the tables laid out for that. We see every sort of Fable crowded together at dozens of long tables and maybe see Snow mooshing some wedding cake all over Bigby's face. It's a joyous scene.

Cap: So they feasted.

Panel Three

The feast continues. A slightly drunken Boy Blue stands up to deliver the traditional Best Man's toast.

Cap: And toasted each other.

Boy Blue: To the finest man and finest woman it has been my good fortune to know.

Panel Four

We see Bigby and Snow running off to wherever it is they're going. Rose Red and Boy Blue hold the kids from following. Fly and Red Riding Hood are also in this scene.

Cap: And celebrated the joyous day.

One of the Kids: Where are Mommy and Daddy going now?

Rose Red: Somewhere you're not invited, wolfling.

Riding Hood (to Fly): That's odd. He does seem familiar — as if we'd met before.

Page Forty Seven (four panels)

Panel One

This isn't really a panel. It's the space you need to leave at the top of the page for the final chapter title.

Title (display lettering): Epilogue: Mr. and Mrs. Wolf

Panel Two

We see Paris at night, all lit up.

Cap: No one quite knew where they planned to go on their honeymoon, or how long they might stay away.

Voice (from city): A little more champagne, Mrs. Wolf?

Panel Three

Now we return to daytime and Wolf Valley. In the background we see their new home. It's a wonderful and sprawling one-story thing: part cabin and partly made of dressed stone and lots of real glass windows and stone chimneys and enough rooms so that each kid gets his own room. Mark: Keep in mind that however you design this, you're likely to be drawing it every once in a while, until the end of time. Here and there, away from the house, there are odds and ends of the construction materials still on site, as if it were just finished minutes before the new family arrived. In the foreground we see Bigby and Snow, hand in hand, walking away from us, walking towards the house. Ahead of them the six kids race like hellions towards the house, so that they can be the first to pick their rooms. This is long after the wedding, so Snow and Bigby and all the kids will be dressed differently than when we last saw them.

Cap: But true to Boy Blue's promise, their house in Wolf Valley was finished and waiting for them by the time they returned.

Snow: Go pick your rooms, children. You each have one of your own.

Panel Four

Now the kids have long disappeared into the house's open front door. Bigby has lifted Snow up into his arms to carry her over the threshold.

Snow: So, do you think happily ever after is possible after all?

Bigby: We'll see.

Panel Five

Same exact scene, but now everyone has entered the house and we see the door close behind them, signaling that they have left the series — for now.

No captions or dialogue in this panel.

Page Forty Eight (one panel)

This is a full page splash, leaving only enough room at the bottom of the page, as the final thing on this page, for this issue's title and credits. We are looking down on the surface of one of the feasting tables at Snow and Bigby's wedding. We see a fine plate with some partially-eaten wedding cake on it. We see a crystal champagne flute with some champagne still in it and a lipstick stain on the rim of the glass. We see a little bit of this and that — like a used fork and maybe a few Polaroid snapshots of the wedding and feast that followed. In the center of this untidy scene we see one of the wedding invitations, which reads as follows (in a fine script, please): You are cordially invited to join with us in celebrating the marriage of Snow White to Bigby Wolf. And under that: R.S.V.P.

Title (display lettering in fine script): Happily Ever After

Credits (in the same script)

Cap (not to be repeated in the collected version): The creators and publishers of Fables would like to thank you, our readers, for your loyalty, encouragement and reliable "what happens next" interest in these first fifty issues. We'll see you next month when the next fifty begins.